"If you want a friend who is not afraid to be real, who understands your fears, and who will take you gently by the hand and show you how to feel God's love, you've found her in this book!"

SUSAN YATES

speaker and best-selling author of several books, including *31 Days of Prayer for My Teen*

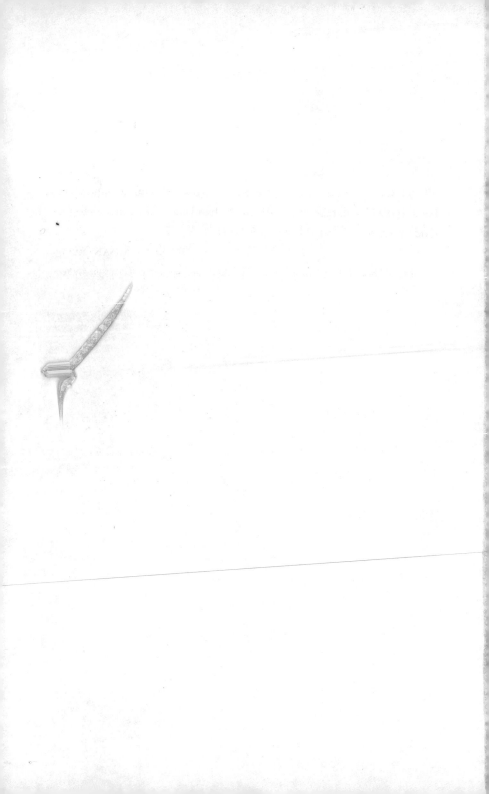

FINDING CALM IN LIFE'S CHAOS

SAFE SHELTER *in the* ARMS OF JESUS

BECKY HARLING

NAVPRESS®

BRINGING TRUTH TO LIFE

OUR GUARANTEE TO YOU

We believe so strongly in the message of our books that we are making this quality guarantee to you. If for any reason you are disappointed with the content of this book, return the title page to us with your name and address and we will refund to you the list price of the book. To help us serve you better, please briefly describe why you were disappointed. Mail your refund request to: NavPress, P.O. Box 35002, Colorado Springs, CO 80935.

The Navigators is an international Christian organization. Our mission is to reach, disciple, and equip people to know Christ and to make Him known through successive generations. We envision multitudes of diverse people in the United States and every other nation who have a passionate love for Christ, live a lifestyle of sharing Christ's love, and multiply spiritual laborers among those without Christ.

NavPress is the publishing ministry of The Navigators. NavPress publications help believers learn biblical truth and apply what they learn to their lives and ministries. Our mission is to stimulate spiritual formation among our readers.

ISBN 1-57683-619-3

Cover design by studiogearbox.com
Cover image by David Pu'u/Corbis
Creative Team: Rachelle Gardner, Liz Heaney, Arvid Wallen, Kathy Mosier, Glynese Northam

All stories in this book are true and have been used with verbal permission. Unless the individual requested otherwise, all names and some identifying circumstances have been changed in order to protect privacy.

Unless otherwise identified, all Scripture quotations in this publication are taken from the HOLY BIBLE: NEW INTERNATIONAL VERSION® (NIV®). Copyright © 1973, 1978, 1984 by International Bible Society. Used by permission of Zondervan Publishing House. All rights reserved. Other versions used include: the New American Standard Bible (NASB), © The Lockman Foundation 1960, 1962, 1963, 1968, 1971, 1972, 1973, 1975, 1977, 1995; the Revised Standard Version Bible (RSV), copyright 1946, 1952, 1971, by the Division of Christian Education of the National Council of the Churches of Christ in the USA, used by permission, all rights reserved; THE MESSAGE (MSG). Copyright © 1993, 1994, 1995, 1996, 2000, 2001, 2002. Used by permission of NavPress Publishing Group; the Holy Bible, New Living Translation (NLT), copyright © 1996. Used by permission of Tyndale House Publishers, Inc., Wheaton, Illinois 60189. All rights reserved; and the New King James Version (NKJV). Copyright © 1982 by Thomas Nelson, Inc. Used by permission. All rights reserved.

Harling, Becky, 1957-
  Finding calm in life's chaos : safe shelter in the arms of Jesus / Becky Harling.-- 1st ed.
     p. cm.
  Includes bibliographical references.
  ISBN 1-57683-619-3
  1. Consolation. 2. Trust in God. 3. Jesus Christ--Words. I. Title.
BV4909.H365 2005
232.9'54--dc22
                             2005002749
Printed in Canada

1 2 3 4 5 6 7 8 9 10 / 09 08 07 06 05

FOR A FREE CATALOG OF
NAVPRESS BOOKS & BIBLE STUDIES,
CALL 1-800-366-7788 (USA)
OR 1-800-839-4769 (CANADA)

To Steve, my beloved husband.
In addition to loving me, you have taught me
how to communicate God's Word with passion and poise.

To Linda Dillow, my precious mentor.
You have taught me how to nestle down deeply
into the safe shelter of His holy presence. I will be forever
indebted to you for your love, counsel, and wisdom.

CONTENTS

FOREWORD

What are the qualifications necessary to write a book about finding calm in chaos? First, you have to experience lots of pain. Becky qualifies. Next, you have to mix the pain with years of turmoil and uncertainty. Becky qualifies. But most important of all, you must find peace in the midst of panic and calm in your chaos. Becky qualifies. I know. I have walked every step of the journey with her.

I remember the day we met. Immediately I was drawn to the petite woman with the beautiful, expressive blue eyes. We sat across from one another having lunch, and within the first half hour, Becky, a pastor's wife and women's ministry director, asked, "Linda, will you mentor me?" I lived in Colorado and Becky lived in Rochester, New York. Mentoring by long distance was not something I relished, and I always pray about a request like this . . . yet I heard myself saying, "Yes." This simple yes began one of the most beautiful relationships in my life.

Perhaps you are asking, "What is a spiritual mentor?" Richard Foster describes it like this: "Spiritual mentors are people gifted in discernment, wisdom, and knowledge. Their task is to help people see the footprints of God in their lives and, now and again, to urge them to move in directions that they might not go otherwise."[1] I have been privileged to be Becky's mentor, yet during these five years, she has imparted wisdom and encouragement to me! Rarely do we have the joy and privilege of seeing deeply into someone's life, of knowing her on a "soul" level. I have had this privilege with Becky.

Two months after I met Becky, she was diagnosed with breast cancer. A double mastectomy began a long parade of trials that marched through her life with a deafening drumbeat. And with each new disaster, the drums beat louder. Most women would have crashed with the first sound of tragedy, but not Becky. Her focus stayed fixed on Jesus, and her feet were planted firmly in His footprints. I watched when the pressure was so great that Becky could not stand; she learned to fall to her knees in worship. I cried with her when yet one more crash of the cymbals sounded; she pressed deeper into the great I AM.

I begged God to stop the chaotic drumbeat, and He said, "Becky is mine. I am crafting a jewel." And He has. Becky has truly discovered Him as her safe shelter in the midst of pain and chaos. I have learned from watching Becky, and now you can too!

Becky's book is titled *Finding Calm in Life's Chaos*. As she has written and shared her story with you, the chaotic drumbeat has continued. Becky writes with authenticity because she is authentic — she continues to live with uncertainty and pain as she writes of victory! Becky will act as a mentor as she teaches you about how the only safe shelter in the chaos of life is found in the arms of Jesus.

No matter what crazy chaos is marching through your life, if you feel as if the beating drums of pain will engulf you, Becky will show you the way out of your chaos by leading you to the safe shelter of Jesus through His incredible "I am" statements. You will learn how to hide in Him when you're petrified, how to find hope in Him when you see and feel no hope. And perhaps best of all, you will learn how to find His presence in worship.

I am no longer just Becky's spiritual mentor. I have become her intimate friend and feel such pride in the person she has become. I highly recommend this book to you. Let Becky take you by the hand and guide you. I am convinced that if you will come to these pages and ask God to open the eyes of your heart, if you will read prayerfully and work through the twelve-week Bible study, you *will* discover a beautiful calm in the midst of your chaos!

LINDA DILLOW
Author of *Calm My Anxious Heart*

ACKNOWLEDGMENTS

A special thanks to:

My precious children, Bethany, Josiah, Stefanie, and Kerith: Thank you for cheering me on as I wrote and modeling joy and laughter for me, even in the midst of chaos. I love you!

My dear friend Jill: Thank you for your prayers and friendship and for sharing your home so that I could write away from the chaos of my own home.

My mother: Thank you for giving me an early introduction to Jesus and a love for books.

My godly counselor and friend, Kris: Thank you for your gentleness and wisdom in my life.

My incredible editor, Liz Heaney: Thank you for your wonderful encouragement and wisdom throughout this project. Without you, I never could have done this!

The women in my small group: Thank you for field-testing this book with me. Our times together were precious to me.

Marian Eberly: Thank you for sharing your wise comments on eating disorders.

And to the men and women at NavPress: What a privilege to be published by you!

CHAPTER 1

NOWHERE TO RUN, NOWHERE TO HIDE

I scanned the small sanctuary, planning my escape route. I knew my stomach couldn't hang on much longer. Earlier that morning I had called my fiancé, Steve, explaining that I had the flu and didn't think it wise for me to go with him to the church considering him for the position of pastor. I rationalized that it was unlikely they would vote him in, considering they had already turned down thirteen other potential pastors, but the bottom line was that I felt sicker than a dog. But Steve, nervous about the whole process, had begged over the phone, "Oh, honey, please. You are my fiancée. They need to meet you. After all, you might become their pastor's wife." So I complied against my better judgment. Trust me, we both regretted that decision!

I now found myself feeling nauseated, trapped in a morning worship service and nervously searching for a way out. When Steve began praying the pastoral prayer, I saw my chance to escape. Checking to be sure that every head was bowed and every eye closed, I clutched my stomach and headed for the nearest exit. But I never made it out of that small country church. Eyes popped and mouths dropped as I lost my breakfast all over the front of the sanctuary. The only eyes closed were those of my future husband, who kept right on praying.

Humiliated and embarrassed, I wanted to crawl away and hide.

Amazingly, that congregation voted us in unanimously. To this day, Steve calls it a "pity vote."

CHASING THE WIND

A few months later, Steve and I moved into the parsonage next to the church. As a young pastor's wife, I told myself I had to "run faster, jump higher, and try harder." These messages were not new; they had been a part of my life since childhood. I had grown up trying to keep others happy; now I had an entire congregation to keep happy.

Determined to do things right, I set my heart to learn all I could about being a dedicated wife and ministry partner. I read every book I could find on parenting techniques and creating a godly home. As opportunities came to teach the Word of God, I studied all the popular books on communicating with poise and passion. Later, as new positions brought bigger challenges, I devoured books on honing leadership skills. Yet perpetual, internal striving left me feeling stressed out, exhausted, and trapped. Nothing I did seemed to lessen the tension and anxiety I felt. I spent my energy trying to do all the things I thought I was supposed to do in order to please God, when in reality I was exhausting myself trying to please others. Though to many I appeared confident and poised, underneath the surface of that well-maintained composure lay some fragile roots, roots that could be easily upturned if life ever felt out of control and chaotic.

SHATTERED DREAMS

Ten years ago, the storm winds of chaos blew into my life, shaking me to the core and forcing me to take an honest look at myself and my relationship with God. I stood by helplessly as one dream after another disintegrated. Several serious issues rocked my world. My teenage daughter struggled with an eating disorder, and in the process of trying to help her, I realized I had the greater problem. The guilt I felt shattered any illusions I had once entertained of being a good mother. As I entered counseling to deal with my eating issues, God unlocked the doors of childhood trauma, forcing me to come face-to-face with the phantom roots of my fear.

As if my life were not filled with enough stress, a routine mammogram revealed that I had breast cancer, and I went through a complete double mastectomy. The year following the initial surgery, my time was spent going to doctor's appointments and undergoing several reconstructive surgeries. I had very little energy and spiraled into discouragement. All the dreams I had once entertained of changing the world dissolved in puddles of tears on my couch.

During that year, God called Steve and me to a new and larger ministry clear across the country. Everything in me panicked. *Now, Lord? I'm not ready! I can't step into a bigger ministry now!* But one month after my final surgery, we uprooted our family and kissed security good-bye. We left behind on the East Coast two college-age children and dear friends from the church we'd served for eleven years and moved to California with our two younger daughters to what we perceived to be our dream job.

However, that dream exploded as well. I watched in shock and disbelief as my husband endured continual attacks of criticism. Watching him suffer at the hands of very powerful people felt worse than any of the trauma I had already experienced. Broken and longing for a sense of renewal, Steve resigned. Shortly after his resignation, a routine ultrasound indicated a strong likelihood that I had ovarian cancer, and once again I was scheduled for surgery.

Toward the beginning of all these crises, I felt as though God had abandoned me. He certainly wasn't behaving like the God I had always served. I felt as if everything I had staked my faith on was now up for grabs. Then as the chaos increased, I became more desperate than ever to understand this God whom I said I wanted to serve. Not knowing where else to turn, I cried out to Him in complete and utter desperation, "God, I don't understand Your ways. I thought I knew You, but You have stripped my world bare. I beg You, Lord, show me who You really are. How can I serve You if I'm not even sure I trust You anymore?"

Soon after that prayer, I came across the following passage in Jeremiah:

> But blessed is the woman who trusts in the LORD,
>> whose confidence is in him.
> She will be like a tree planted by the water
>> that sends out its roots by the stream.
> She will not fear when heat comes;
>> her leaves are always green.
> She has no worries in a year of drought
>> and never fails to bear fruit. (17:7-8, author's paraphrase)

Oh, how I wanted to be like this person! Unlike me, she didn't appear frazzled, anxious, or uptight. She remained steady and unshaken, regardless of what came her way. She had no worries. I had plenty. I did not lack spiritual passion or zeal, but despite my best efforts, I felt more like a weeping willow than a sturdy oak tree.

Convinced that some of the answers I was seeking lay in this passage, I determined to study it more. As I studied, God began to show me why it was difficult for me to trust Him. For many years, I had served God out of fear. But in my fear, I had missed the deeper joy of knowing Him.

In all my striving, I had missed the most important phrase in Jeremiah's description: "whose confidence is in him." This person was calm in the midst of chaos because she willingly placed her trust in God and His character rather than in herself or her circumstances. She was deeply rooted in God, not because she knew about His character or was driven to perform for Him but because she had learned to experience and enjoy Him as her safe shelter. What she knew in her head had somehow made it down into the crevices of her heart. As a result, her confidence in Him had given her everything I longed for—the courage to face challenges, the confidence to feel secure, and the centering peace that all is well. Now the question I faced became *How?* How could I move my head knowledge of God down into the depths of my quaking heart?

I determined to bury myself in the heart of Jesus. For four years straight I read and reread the Gospels, seeking to know Him better. As I studied Jesus' life, His "I am" statements drew me like a magnet. I discovered that every "I am" statement correlates with a significant emotional need. As I began to understand who Jesus was and what He promised through His "I am" statements, I also began to trust Him with a confidence that could not be shaken. As I learned to draw from His character and nestle down in His presence, anxiety was replaced with calmness, panic with confidence, and insecurity with assurance.

While I still don't have this down perfectly, I am *learning* to retreat into His presence moment by moment. I can now follow in the footsteps of Moses and say,

> He who dwells in the shelter of the Most High
> will rest in the shadow of the Almighty.
> I will say of the LORD, "He is my refuge and my fortress,
> my God, in whom I trust." (Psalm 91:1-2)

Courage, confidence, and centering peace ultimately come from steadfast trust in God's holy character and awesome abilities. They are rooted in a belief that has taken up residency in our hearts, the seat of our emotions. When we put our trust in God, we realize that we cannot do it alone. Therefore,

> Let not the wise man boast of his wisdom
> or the strong man boast of his strength
> or the rich man boast of his riches,
> but let him who boasts boast about this:

that he understands and knows me.
(Jeremiah 9:23-24)

God never fails, never changes, never grows weary, and never quits. When we trust in His character and abilities, we can rest because He is ever-present and everything we need. Change doesn't seem as daunting. Difficulties don't seem so monumental. Disappointments hurt but don't diffuse all hope. Instead, the woman who knows God intimately is able to face life's chaos with assurance, security, strength, and hope because her tranquility flows out of the glorious character of Almighty God.

The book you now hold in your hands is the result of my study and of my hours spent in His presence. As you read about Jesus and study His "I am" statements —

"I am . . . he"
"I am the bread of life"
"I am the light of the world"
"I am the good shepherd"
"I am the resurrection and the life"
"I am the way"
"I am . . . the truth"
"I am the vine"
"I am the Alpha and the Omega" —

I pray that you will find yourself drawn into God's presence and that you will come to know Him more intimately.

WHERE DO YOU HIDE?

Wherever you are with God at this moment, it's possible to go deeper. Is He the One you turn to when life leaves you wounded, torn apart, and stripped? Perhaps you've become disillusioned with Him and now wonder if you ever really knew Him. It is even possible that He is the One you are blaming for your chaos. Maybe your world is rocking at this very moment; maybe the winds of chaos are blowing. Where are you planning to hide?

The Almighty God who created you understands you perfectly. He wants you to know Him, not just casually but intimately. Will you lay aside any preconceived notions you might have about Him and join me as an inquisitive child, seeking only to know the truth about His character?

If you put His promises to the test, I dare say that you won't be disappointed. If you run to Him who is your safe shelter, you will discover the unshakable peace and security found there.

CHAPTER 2

WHERE CAN I DUMP MY BUCKET OF GUILT?

"I who speak to you am he."
JOHN 4:26

*I*f women could buy a guilt eraser at the cosmetic counter, local department stores would be sold out because so many of us feel guilty.

Sandy lies in bed at night feeling guilty for losing her cool with her kids — again.

Stephanie feels that if people really knew her, they would no longer respect and like her.

Tara has done some things in her life that she feels too ashamed to talk about with anyone.

Shannon constantly berates herself for not living up to her own ideals.

Lenore cringes every time she drives past Weight Watchers — she's rejoined at least four times.

Corrine feels as though the word divorce is stamped on her forehead and is overcome by a wave of shame every time she hears a sermon on marriage.

No matter why we feel guilty, most of us will agree on one thing: We feel guilty. And we are guilty. Because to be guilty means we have done something wrong. And let's face it, we've all messed up at least once or twice.

If you are thinking, *Hey wait a minute, Becky, that's not the answer I was looking for! I was hoping this chapter would help me get rid of my guilt!*, please hear me out. I promise you, I'll show you what to do about getting rid of your guilt.

THE ANSWER TO OUR GUILT

All of us are guilty in God's eyes because His standard is complete holiness. No matter how hard we try, we can't measure up. All of us are guilty of breaking God's laws and "fall short" of His holy standards (Romans 3:23). That's the bad news.

The good news is that Jesus came as the answer to our guilt. He emphatically claimed to have "authority on earth to forgive sins" (Luke 5:24). He came as the Messiah not to shame us but to gently and honestly reveal our sin and then to offer us forgiveness and cleansing.

The apostle John records the story of a woman who carried a bucket full of guilt (see 4:7-42). She had looked for love in all the wrong places and made many poor choices along the way. Jesus met her at the well in Samaria and didn't condemn her or shame her, although He could have. Instead, He lovingly confronted her sin and then offered a solution — not a quick spray of Guilt Away but the opportunity to receive the living water of salvation, which would absolve her of guilt. In the course of their conversation, He told her, "I . . . am he." This is the first "I am" statement that Jesus made, and He made it to a woman! By claiming, "I am he," Jesus identified Himself as the Messiah. As such, He had come to save her not only from the political oppression she experienced as a Samaritan and a woman but also from the oppression of sin. Let's take a look at this story to see what implications there might be for those of us struggling with guilt.

SHACKLED BY THE PAST

As the scene unfolds, we find Jesus, tired from His journey, sitting all alone at the well in Samaria. While He rests, a woman comes to draw water. Jesus asks her, "Will you give me a drink?" (verse 7).

Shocked, the woman bristles and says, "You are a Jew and I am a Samaritan *woman*. How can *you* ask *me* for a drink?" verse 9, (emphasis added). She must have been wondering, *Who is this guy, and why is he talking to me?*

Most women traveled to the well in groups early in the morning or late in the evening in order to avoid the heat, but this woman made the trek alone in the heat of the day. Why? I think it's possible that she went alone so she wouldn't have to deal with the judgmental scorn of the other women in town. We discover later in the passage (verses 17-18) that this woman's reputation wasn't exactly squeaky clean.

Jesus, however, looks behind her self-protective behavior and gently addresses her deepest need. He tells her, "If you knew the gift of God and who it is that asks you for a drink, you would have asked him and he would have given you living water."

Immediately intrigued, she asks for living water so she won't have to keep making the daily hike to the well. But Jesus continues to probe, saying, "Go, call your husband and come back."

Nervously she stammers, "I have no husband."

With infinite wisdom and divine compassion, Jesus places His finger on the sin that she would rather have left hidden and tells her, "You are right when you say you have no husband. The fact is, you have had five husbands, and the man you now have is not your husband." Ouch!

What could she say? What would you say if you were her? Would you quickly change the topic to divert His attention? Feeling guilty, that's exactly what she did. She has been around the block a few times and is pretty good at fast thinking, so she steers the conversation to worship. A nice safe topic in anyone's book, unless of course you happen to be talking to Jesus, the Son of God. He explains that it's not *where* you worship but *who* and *how* you worship that count. He tells her, "God is spirit, and his worshipers must worship in spirit and in truth."

She then says, "I know that Messiah is coming. When he comes, he will explain everything to us." Her unspoken question is, *Are you the Messiah?*

Bingo! She's finally got it!

Jesus, reading her thoughts, speaks gently, letting the truth wash over her soul, "I who speak to you am he."

WHO NEEDS A MESSIAH?

As the Messiah, Jesus was the only one who could fulfill her longings and take away her guilt. He had come to her in the chaos of her life to rescue her and offer her a safe shelter from guilt. This would be good news for one who had much to feel guilt over! Other religious leaders might tell her she was not good enough or that she would have to earn freedom from guilt, but not Jesus. He had come with a different agenda. He was not what she expected.

For one thing, the Jews hated the Samaritans because they were "half-breeds,"[1] yet Jesus was kind to her. For another, this "Messiah" had no army or royal entourage. As a Samaritan, she likely expected a Messiah who would come in power and rescue her people. She would have expected the Messiah to be "someone who would be a political liberator."[2] Instead, Jesus lived a humble, simple life. He came to liberate the world from sin and guilt, not from oppressive governments.

So in keeping with His mission, Jesus told the Samaritan woman, "The [living] water I give [you] will become in [you] a spring of water welling up to eternal life" (John 4:14). The picture here is of a fountain of pure water continually gushing up within us — available, accessible, and abundant. Once received, it springs up, purifying our hearts and making us whole for all eternity. Paul referred to this cleansing when he wrote, "But you were washed, you were sanctified" (1 Corinthians 6:11).

Jesus invites, "Come! . . . Whoever wishes, let him take the free gift of the water of life" (Revelation 22:17). Drawing water from a well is hard work, but the living water Jesus promises is a free gift. It can't be earned. It must simply be received.

The Bible tells us that our sin separates us from God and must be punished (see Isaiah 59:2). That is why we need a Messiah, someone to liberate us from our sin. Jesus came and took the punishment for our wrong choices by dying on the cross. He accomplished the forgiveness of our sins by becoming our guilt offering (see Isaiah 53:10; Acts 5:31). Why would He do such a thing? Because He loves us and wants a relationship with us. When we receive His living water, He washes away our guilt and restores our relationship with Him.

If you have not received His living water, would you like to? Would you like to be made completely clean? You can by admitting you have sinned, repenting (telling God you are sorry and then turning from your sin), and receiving Him into your life. You can receive Him right now through prayer, which is talking to God. You might want to make up your own prayer, or you can use the prayer below. What matters to God is the sincerity of your heart.

> *Dear Lord Jesus, I know that I am a sinner and need Your forgiveness. Thank You for dying for my sins. I want to turn from my sins and be made clean. Please come into my heart and life. I want to receive Your living water and follow You as Lord and Savior. Amen.*

If you prayed that prayer, you are now God's precious child. The Bible tells us that "to all who received him, to those who believed in his name, he gave the right to become children of God" (John 1:12). He has become your personal Messiah. His living water is continually available and always accessible to "sanctify you through and through" (1 Thessalonians 5:23).

He will never take away His living water, even if you sin. You are forever guilt free.

THEN WHY DO I STILL FEEL GUILTY?

Even so, if you are like many women I know, you still struggle with guilt. If the living water of salvation washes away our guilt, then why do we still feel guilty at times?

When a Christian feels guilty, it's usually for one of four reasons:

- We have sinned by disobeying God in some way, and our relationship with Him has become strained due to a breech in our rapport with Him. The Holy Spirit acts as an alarm, letting us know when we sin so that we can restore broken fellowship with God once again. He does this by pricking our conscience so that we feel guilty. We can then recognize that we have sinned and seek reconciliation. The guilt we feel is appropriate and true.

- We are unable to forgive ourselves for a particular sin (even though we have confessed it and God has forgiven us). The guilt we feel in this case is inappropriate and false.

- We have not met our own or someone else's standards. The guilt we feel is inappropriate and false.

- We have absorbed someone else's guilt for evil done to us. The guilt we feel is inappropriate and false.

In other words, guilt felt *before* repentance is the conviction of the Holy Spirit, but guilt felt *after* repentance is condemnation and does not come from God. Condemnation is *never* God's plan for His children (see Romans 8:1). His desire is that we experience the freedom of His forgiveness and enjoy fellowship with Him.

WHEN A CHRISTIAN SINS . . .

The Holy Spirit doesn't convict us of sin in order to make us miserable. Rather, He pricks our conscience so that we will repent, turn from sin, and reestablish our fellowship with God. That is the purpose of guilt. Biblical repentance calls us to a change of heart and attitude. It brings our spirit into alignment with the Holy Spirit. We see this in King David's life.

David, though called a man after God's own heart (see Acts 13:22), committed the sins of adultery and murder. When the prophet Nathan confronted David about his sin, David knew he was guilty of violating God's laws. He recognized that he had done evil in God's sight, and he repented, praying, "Wash away all my iniquity and cleanse me from my sin" (Psalm 51:2). The Hebrew word David chose for *wash* here refers to a thorough cleansing both inside and out, a cleansing that "pervades the substance of the thing washed."[3] God heard David's prayer for mercy and forgave him, cleansing him completely and restoring their relationship.

The Holy Spirit used the prophet Nathan to convict David of his sin. He used a movie to convict my friend Lorraine. She says,

> One Sunday our pastor showed a video of an eight-week-old fetus. I was appalled as I watched a hand move and a foot kick. When I had my abortion years before, I had been told that the doctor was removing only a "blob of tissue." Now, my selfish choice hit me. Watching that movie, I saw my actions through God's eyes — as sin. That afternoon I fell on my knees and while weeping confessed, "Forgive me, God. I killed my baby."

God forgave Lorraine completely. She now ministers hope and healing to other women who have aborted their babies by assuring them that God's forgiveness is complete.

Do you find Lorraine's story hard to believe? Do you feel that some sins are just too big or too heinous for God to forgive? This is simply not true! God forgives any sin we repent of, no matter how significant or heinous. Our guilt is completely wiped away. He tells us in His Word,

> But if we confess our sins to him, he is faithful and just to forgive us and to cleanse us from every wrong. (1 John 1:9, NLT)

> "But I, yes I, am the one
>   who takes care of your sins — that's what I do.
>   I don't keep a list of your sins." (Isaiah 43:25, MSG)

> "Though your sins are as scarlet,
>   They will be as white as snow;
> Though they are red like crimson,
>   They will be like wool." (Isaiah 1:18, NASB)

> "I will sprinkle clean water upon you, and you shall be clean from all your uncleannesses, and from all your idols I will cleanse you. A new heart I will give you, and a new spirit I will put within you; and I will take out of your flesh the heart of stone and give you a heart of flesh. And I will put my spirit within you, and cause you to walk in my statutes and be careful to observe my ordinances. You shall dwell in the land which I gave to your fathers; and you shall be my people, and I will be your God." (Ezekiel 36:25-29, RSV)

God never turns away a repentant sinner. Not once in all of Scripture does He turn away one who repents. It would be inconsistent with His character to do so! So if you have asked God to forgive you of a sin, He has forgiven you. Trust that He has emptied your bucket of true guilt and filled it with the living water of forgiveness. God does what He says He will do.

While true guilt leads to repentance, forgiveness, and the restoration of our fellowship with God, false guilt leads to beating ourselves up and bondage.

IDENTIFYING FALSE GUILT

Satan, "the accuser" (Revelation 12:10), loves to get us all tied up in guilt because guilt keeps us from enjoying the freedom of Christ's finished work. Let's take a closer look at three of his favorite strategies.

GUILT OVER SIN ALREADY CONFESSED

During her early twenties, Doreen had been sexually promiscuous and had experimented with drugs. Although she had confessed this to the Lord many times, she could not shake that unclean feeling.

When she came to me for help, I reminded Doreen of 1 John 1:9: "If we confess our sins, he is faithful and just and will forgive us our sins and purify us from *all* unrighteousness" (emphasis added). While Doreen knew these words, she had never allowed them to sink deeply into her heart. Together we got on our knees, and I listened as Doreen once again confessed her past sins. But this time I encouraged her to quote 1 John 1:9, claiming it by faith over each and every sin. I acted as her witness. I heard her confess each sin and trust by faith that she had received Christ's forgiveness for all of them.

In the front cover of her Bible she wrote, "I am clean. My past has been forgiven. I no longer have to carry my guilt. Jesus has taken it away." Next to Doreen's statement I wrote the date, and together we signed our

31

names. The next time Doreen felt guilty, she could look at that statement and remind herself that she had been forgiven and made clean.

Do Doreen's feelings sound familiar? I've met many women who feel guilty over sin already confessed. Perhaps for you the sin is not drugs or sexual promiscuity but a lie you told or jealousy you felt or gossip you shared. You've confessed, but you still feel guilty. Please believe me when I say that this is *not* God's will for you. One of the Enemy's favorite tactics is to torment you with past sin so that you will not experience the full measure of Christ's forgiveness. Remember, Jesus has all authority to forgive sins (see Luke 5:24). If you have repented, He has removed your sins far from you (see Psalm 103:12).

GUILT OVER UNREALISTIC EXPECTATIONS

With the many different roles and relationships women juggle, it is easy for those of us who are people-pleasers to feel false guilt when we disappoint others or ourselves. Consider the following examples:

- Your schedule is busy. Time is at a premium, and you are trying to juggle your job, your marriage, your children, and your friends. A friend wants more time with you and expresses hurt feelings because she feels that you never make time for her. You feel guilty because she thinks you aren't being a good friend.

- Your definition of being a "good mother" means attending every activity your children are involved in. When an unexpected meeting comes up at work and you cannot make an event, you beat yourself up for not being a good parent.

- Your mother always had a clean house and homemade cookies. You, on the other hand, are the first to volunteer in your community, and as a result, the laundry rarely gets folded and Oreos are the closest thing to a homemade cookie you ever serve. When your mother comes over you feel bad, wondering why you can't get your life organized.

- Other parents in your church send their children to private Christian schools or homeschool their kids. But you can't afford private schooling, and homeschooling is *way* out of your comfort zone. Still, every time you see those other families, you fear you may be doing your child a disservice.

GUILT OVER EVIL ABSORBED

While guilt over expectations is troubling, more difficult by far is the guilt we feel over absorbed evil. Let me explain. I had just finished speaking and had invited the audience to come forward for prayer. As I stood with my head bowed waiting for those who might come, Carla approached me in tears. I held her and stroked her hair as she cried, "I am so dirty! Why would God want me? Why would He want me?"

When Carla's sobs grew quiet, her story came out in broken pieces. Carla had been raped as a young teenager, and she struggled with ongoing feelings of guilt and shame over what had happened to her. Rather than seeing her attacker as evil, she had absorbed the evil committed against her. As a result, she had never felt "clean," even though she had done nothing wrong.

I gently explained to her that she had carried a heavy load of guilt all these years over sin that was not hers. She was not guilty of any wrongdoing in God's eyes. I told her that Jesus longed to heal her wounds, not punish her for them. The relief in her eyes told me that Carla needed to hear categorically from another Christian woman that being a victim of rape was not a sin.

As we prayed together, Carla told God about the hurt that the rape had caused her. She also acknowledged that the rape had been someone else's evil choice and asked the holy Healer to remove the residual feelings of uncleanness she had carried for so long. Carla also agreed to see a

Christian counselor who specializes in the issues resulting from rape.

Of course, rape is not the only evil that women can absorb. We can also blame ourselves for such things as childhood sexual or physical abuse or for wife battering. Such issues are complex, and complete healing often takes time and professional help. But be assured that whatever the reason you may have absorbed someone else's guilt, it is not God's will for you to carry that heavy load!

IT'S TIME TO DUMP *YOUR* GUILT BUCKET

It's possible that as you've read this chapter, you've realized you need to do some dumping! Your guilt bucket is getting pretty heavy. Lorraine, Carla, Doreen, and I have all dumped ours — and we're committed to keep dumping. How about you? Are you tired of carrying that heavy load? Are you ready to dump your guilt? To do so, keep a "guilt journal" for a week. Write down every time you feel guilty and then analyze your list, identifying the reasons you feel guilty by asking yourself these four questions:

1. *Have I disobeyed God in some way?* If you have, confess and ask God for godly sorrow. What you confess, God will forgive (see 1 John 1:9).

2. *Have I already asked God to forgive me for this sin?* If so, do not accept any of Satan's accusations but instead claim the lordship of Jesus Christ over those feelings and cling for all you are worth to the truth taught in God's Word. Consider doing what Doreen did and confess your sin once again in front of a witness. God has already forgiven you, but this will allow you to have the reassurance of a witness and may help you *feel* forgiven. Make a covenant and date the moment with a witness so that you have a record of finding forgiveness over that particular sin. If guilt resurfaces, you will have tangible proof that you have no reason to feel guilty.

3. *Am I feeling disappointed for not measuring up to the ideal woman I or someone else thinks I should be?* If you answer yes to this question, you might be helped by looking at how Jesus responded to other people's expectations of Him. For example, in Mark 1:35-39 the disciples told Jesus, who had been spending time alone with the Father, "Everyone is looking for you!" In other words, "How dare you take time to be by yourself when there are more people waiting to be healed?" Jesus, however, calmly responded, "Let us go somewhere else . . . so I can preach there also. That is why I have come." He didn't seem the least bit worried about what the people or even the disciples might think. Why? Because He knew what His priorities were, and as long as He was attending to them, He was doing what the Father wanted. His purpose on earth was not to make others happy. Neither is ours.

While it's not easy to dump unrealistic expectations, here are a few suggestions that might help:

- Make a list of your priorities. Evaluate the things that make you feel guilty by comparing them to the items on your list and remind yourself that Jesus does not expect you to make other people happy. Here's how this helps me. My top priorities are:

  ❏ Cultivating my relationship with Jesus Christ

  ❏ Cultivating my relationship with my husband

  ❏ Cultivating my relationship with my children

  ❏ Cultivating a few close friendships

  ❏ Cultivating my ministry of helping women go deeper in

their relationship with Christ through speaking, writing, and mentoring

❑ Cultivating casual friendships and community involvement

When I feel guilty for not living up to someone's expectations, I refer to this list. I remember that my top three priorities will take the most of my time. The other three priorities are a juggling act. My close friends understand my heart for ministry. When someone suggests other opportunities for involvement in my community, I always pray about those opportunities, but I allow my priorities to guide my thinking. I can't be all things to all people, and there are only twenty-four hours in a day. My list of priorities helps me dump any guilt I might feel over saying no.

• Take responsibility for your own actions. The flip side of not taking responsibility for others' happiness is to take responsibility for your own. Make two lists on a piece of paper. On one side list what you can take responsibility for; on the other side list what you cannot control. For example:

❑ I can be responsible for having time with the Lord every day.

❑ I can take responsibility for my own attitude.

❑ I can take responsibility for making a good dinner at night and doing the laundry regularly or delegating these tasks.

❑ I cannot be responsible if my teenager is angry at me because I said no to a request.

❑ I cannot be responsible for my husband's grouchiness over losing his cell phone.

❑ I cannot take responsibility for my friend's hurt feelings if my child gets sick and I have to cancel plans.

- If your struggle is living up to your own expectations, enlist some help. Ask a mature Christian friend or your husband to help you give up trying to be "superwoman" and figure out how to lower the bar.

  I benefited from this recently when I was feeling guilty for missing one of my child's sporting events. I felt so bad that I was in tears. Steve took one look at me and asked if I felt it was realistic to attend every event of every one of our four children. He then reminded me that *he* had gone to the sporting event and that our child had done just fine — and was now in bed peacefully sleeping while I was crying and unable to sleep! Steve helped me see that my expectations were unrealistic, and that enabled me to dump my bucket of false guilt.

- Apologize only once. This principle applies to true and false guilt and is a healthy pattern for life. If you sin, repent and apologize to the Lord once. He doesn't call you to beat yourself up. If you hurt another person, take responsibility and apologize once. If you disappoint someone and truly feel sorry, apologize once.

  Apologizing over and over is a form of self-punishment. Once is enough. When we beat ourselves up, we don't honor Christ. He took the punishment for our sins so that we wouldn't have to.

4. *Have I absorbed guilt from evil committed against me?* If you are struggling with guilt for evil done to you, particularly if you were raped or suffered some other kind of abuse, I strongly urge you to seek help from a professional, godly therapist.

While the importance of professional help cannot be overstated, you can do some tangible things to help you focus on the truth that you have no reason to feel guilty. For example:

- Memorize some verses that remind you that God does not see you as guilty. When the guilt feelings come, pray and claim those Scriptures over them. Here are two to get you started:

  > Therefore, there is now no condemnation for those who are in Christ Jesus. (Romans 8:1)

  > No, in all these things [even guilt feelings] we are more than conquerors through him who loved us. For I am convinced that neither death nor life, neither angels nor demons, neither the present nor the future, nor any powers . . . will be able to separate us from the love of God that is in Christ Jesus our Lord. (Romans 8:37-39)

- Find a visual symbol that will remind you that you are clean in God's eyes. For example, Kristen has a white towel hanging in her closet as a symbol that the sexual abuse committed against her as a child was not her fault and that she is clean. Shelly wears a cross that reminds her that the rape she survived was not her fault. When guilt sabotages her peace, Shelly momentarily feels the cross and immediately thanks Jesus for rescuing her from her feelings of uncleanness.

God never intended you to feel guilty for someone else's evil. He sent Jesus, your Messiah, to rescue you from the oppression of these feelings. Jesus absorbed your perpetrator's guilt so you wouldn't have to. Allow Him to free you from that burden. Seek the help of a professional, godly counselor. Pray back Scripture every time guilt sabotages your peace and choose a symbol as a reminder that you are clean and free.

Christ came to save you from sin and the punishment of that sin. The moment you receive His living water of salvation, you are given the lifelong solution to guilt: His Holy Spirit. He is your internal cleansing agent. Listen to His voice when you feel guilty. He will show you the difference between true guilt and false guilt.

Jesus wants you to experience the joy of His deep cleansing. He speaks to you the same words He spoke to the woman at the well: "I am he, your Messiah."

CHAPTER 3

I WANT TO FEEL LOVED!

"I am the bread of life."
JOHN 6:35

Our family loves Christmas traditions, and since moving to San Diego, we have added a new one. The idea originated with our youngest daughter. Moved with compassion for the many homeless people she saw on street corners, Keri wanted our family to reach out to them in a significant way. She thought the homeless needed more than the Christmas cookies, fruit, and McDonald's gift certificates she had collected for us to pass out on Christmas afternoon. Keri wanted each homeless person to experience love; therefore, she directed her siblings to write messages in Christmas cards so that every person who received food would also receive a special card with a message of God's love.

Steve and I were skeptical. Our practical minds reasoned that those in need would not care about some sentimental Christmas card. Boy, were we wrong! As our family visited the homeless on Christmas afternoon, guess what had the greatest impact? The Christmas cards were not only welcomed but also cherished! Many people commented that it had been years since they had received a card from anyone. My daughter had the wisdom to understand what God has known all along: People are hungry for more than just food.

AN INVITATION TO HUNGRY PEOPLE

As Jesus sat teaching on the hillside, a record crowd gathered to listen, enchanted with the rabbi's sermon (see John 6:1-14,26-35). But after a while, twinges of hunger made empty stomachs rumble. One little boy, whose mama had packed him a picnic lunch, sat in the crowd by divine appointment. Andrew, one of Jesus' disciples, noticed the boy's small lunch and pointed it out to Jesus despite his certainty that it wouldn't go far in feeding the large crowd before them. The disciples watched in wonder as Jesus blessed and broke this meager offering. Miraculously, the five small loaves of bread and two tiny fish multiplied, and one small boy's picnic lunch fed the crowd of five thousand who had come to listen to Jesus. (Wouldn't you love to have been there when that little boy returned home and shared the events of the day with his mother?)

Later, the crowd craved more. Not more food — their bellies were full. They longed for another miracle. So they followed Jesus, hoping to catch a glimpse of a second phenomenal show. As they waited, Jesus looked into their hearts and saw the deepest need of the human soul; their hearts were famished for His love. This is exactly why He had come to earth: God sent Jesus to earth as the only One able to completely satisfy the heart's craving for love.

Instead of providing actual food by means of another miracle, Jesus extended an invitation to know Him as the source of all sustenance. He told them, "I am the bread of life. He who comes to me will never go hungry, and he who believes in me will never be thirsty" (John 6:35). Jesus taught that deep within us lies a longing that only He with His infinite, perfect love can satisfy. He promised that those who come to the Bread of Life will never be hungry or thirsty for love again.

SATISFACTION GUARANTEED

A catalog we recently received in the mail assured customers of complete satisfaction with this headline on the front cover: "The Strongest Guarantee in the Business." Jesus knew His listeners needed assurance as well, and He guaranteed complete satisfaction.

How could He make such a promise? The perfection of His nature guarantees the perfection of His love. All of His attributes work together in perfect harmony. God extends His love to us in perfect faithfulness. The book of Psalms often mentions God's love and faithfulness together. The psalmist cries, "Your unfailing love will last forever. Your faithfulness is as enduring as the heavens" (89:2, NLT). David wrote many songs of worship, extolling the Lord's love and faithfulness: "Your love, O LORD, reaches to the heavens, your faithfulness to the skies" (36:5). And "I will bow down toward your holy temple and will praise your name for your love and your faithfulness" (138:2). The love of the Almighty never fails, never disappoints, never diminishes, and never varies. The prophet Jeremiah reminds us that God's love never ceases and that we can experience His mercies as new every morning (see Lamentations 3:22-23).

His perfect love satisfies our longing to be pursued (see Jeremiah 31:3), our desire to be treasured (see Isaiah 62:5), and our need to feel precious (see Isaiah 43:4). How does His love satisfy us like this? He sends His Spirit to live in us so that we have His constant presence continually reassuring us that we are His beloved.

God's love is not only perfect; it is also unlimited. Let's look again at John 6:35: "I am the bread of life. He who comes to me will never go hungry, and he who believes in me will never be thirsty." Notice the word *comes*. In its original Greek form, the word *come* is the present continuous tense.[1] In other words, Jesus is saying, "Don't just come once; keep on coming. The supply of my love never runs out. Feast on my love. Return again and again. If you keep returning for more love, you will never go hungry." We can come to God as often as we need to for love.

This verse reminds me of how I felt as a young mom. My babies' hungry cries stirred in me a longing to meet their need. As I would lift them to my breast, they would frantically root around until their tiny mouths found the source of milk. They would suck in all the milk their little tummies could hold. After they had had their fill, they would grow peaceful and quiet in blissful contentment. After a few hours, though, they would cry for more milk.

What if I had ignored their cries or fed them only once a day? What kind of mother would I have been? My children needed to come to me for milk as soon and as often as they were hungry. So it is with us and our need for God's love. We need to return again and again, hungrily drinking from His love. He promises that the supply will never run out and that He will never forget to feed His children. God tenderly assures,

> "Can a mother forget the baby at her breast
>   and have no compassion on the child she has borne?
> Though she may forget,
>   I will not forget you!" (Isaiah 49:15)

Sometimes we experience God's love through His messages in the Bible. Other times we hear it in the soft whisper of His small voice, reassuring us that He is with us and loves us oh so much. Or we may feel His love descend on us in the form of deep calmness, especially after we have poured out our worries and fears before Him. At times He may give us a vision that shows us how much He loves us. For instance, He has often helped me see myself as a small child nestled in His lap as He tells me over and over how much He loves me. The closer I draw to Him, the more I experience His love.

But I have not always experienced His love, partly because I have looked to others to meet my seemingly insatiable need for love.

MY QUEST FOR LOVE

Early in my marriage I longed for love so much so that my husband told me, "You know, I think you are high maintenance in the love department. I can't possibly meet your needs." This is not something a wife longs to hear! Despite Steve's good intentions, I walked away thinking, *There must be something tragically wrong with me.*

Steve was right. I had a lot of insecurities and needs that no human being could possibly meet. Only Jesus' perfect love could completely satisfy my soul's emptiness. Each of our hearts is like a cup. Sometimes we try to fill our emotional cups with achievement or success or things or even control. I had been trying to fill my emotional cup with the approval and love of individuals: my husband, children, and friends.

I had known God for years, but His perfect love seemed to run through cracks in my soul. Somehow I grew up believing that I deserved to be loved only if I performed well. Consequently, I never felt sure whether God considered my performance quite good enough. Even though I had asked Jesus into my heart, I worried continually, wondering, *What if He keeps a chart with gold stars, and I don't get enough?*

My teachers meant well. They taught me about sin and grace, but I never saw any pictures of God smiling, so I couldn't figure out if He felt happy about giving me grace or if He gave it begrudgingly. Even though I was taught that He loved me, I didn't feel His love for me. On top of that, the thought of a holy God having feelings almost seemed sacrilegious. After all, wouldn't that make Him emotionally weak? It seemed to me that faith was simply an intellectual decision. But if that were true, why did I want so much to feel God's love?

DOES GOD WANT ME TO FEEL HIS LOVE?

In my quest to feel secure in God's love, I sought out a spiritually mature woman who could be a mentor to me in my Christian walk. Linda graciously agreed. At first I felt embarrassed to tell her about my struggle to feel God's love. What would she think? How could I admit that after years of working in full-time ministry, leading others to Christ, and serving in the local church, I still didn't feel loved by God? But I had promised that I'd be honest with her, so after describing how I felt distant from God, I asked her in an e-mail, "Does God want me to feel His love? Are my feelings important?"

Linda returned my e-mail, free of judgment and loaded with confidence:

> Yes! God wants you to feel the pleasure of His love. Bring Him your hunger. He doesn't just want you to know about His love, quote Scriptures about His love, and simply admit with your head that He loves you. His overwhelming desire is for you to *experience* His love. But remember, when you don't feel loved that doesn't mean God's love isn't truth.

Her words pointed out a critical truth: *Our emotions don't dictate the reality of God's love. But God wants the reality of His love to penetrate our emotions.* This is why the apostle Paul prayed this prayer of blessing over his friends in Ephesus:

> May your roots go down deep into the soil of God's marvelous love. And may you have the power to understand, as all God's people should, how wide, how long, how high, and how deep his love really is. May you experience the love of Christ, though it is so great you will never fully understand it. (Ephesians 3:17-19, NLT)

God wants us to go beyond head knowledge of His love; He wants us to feel it. He has designed and wired each of us with emotions and the need to feel loved. He longs for us to live in the safe shelter of His love, to experience being loved from the top of our intellectual head to the bottom of our emotional heart. He invites each of us to come to Him as the Bread of Life and do more than taste. He invites us to savor His love, to fill the deep hunger in our souls with the Bread of Life. Sam Storms says it this way: "He wants you to feel the joy of being loved. He wants you to receive His love personally and powerfully in a way that is life changing."[2] God's love is like an ocean, and He wants us to do more than get our toes wet.

As I walked the beach recently, a little boy about age four helped me understand what this means. Standing near the water's edge, he watched wave after wave roll in and smash against the shore. With each wave, his excitement grew. Finally, he could contain his exuberance no longer. While his older brother cautiously poked his toes in the surf, the four-year-old threw all restraint to the wind. Though fully clothed in pants and a sweatshirt, he took one huge, excited leap and landed with a splash in the waves. Soaked from head to toe, he *experienced* the ocean. And once he did, he could not be stopped. He kept jumping and splashing and running into the waves, delighted and satisfied.

I don't know about you, but that's the way I want to experience Jesus' love. I don't want to stand on the shore and poke my toes in. I don't want to tell myself intellectually that the ocean of God's love exists. No! I want to jump in, get soaking wet, and drink in the pure pleasure of His endless love — and that is precisely what God desires for you and me. He says in effect, "My child, I have oceans of love for you. Don't just look. Don't just affirm by your faith that My love is true. Jump in and experience My love. Let it wash over you completely. Drink deeply until your heart is content."

In order to move my head knowledge of God's love into the deep crevices of my heart, my mentor encouraged me to study about God's love in His Word and write down everything I learned. For one year I did exactly that. Ironically, that was the same year I had surgery for breast cancer, and as a result I had lots of quiet time in His presence. During those months of recovery, I sought God's face, asking Him to help me feel loved by Him. I also read books about experiencing His love and recorded my feelings while reading them. Two books that became personal favorites were *The Satisfied Heart* by Ruth Myers and *The Singing God* by Sam Storms. I read each through several times, asking the Holy Spirit to awaken my soul to Christ's deep love for me.

The Holy Spirit answered my prayer, not only through the books but also through these ways in which He often works:

- Personal worship in my quiet time
- God's love letter, the Word of God
- The love of others
- The sacrament of Communion

FEAST ON HIS LOVE IN WORSHIP

During this journey toward experiencing God's love, I decided to take a day of fasting and prayer. When I told my mentor this, she had a different response: "Oh no, Becky, fasting is not for you." After my initial surprise, I realized God had given Linda great wisdom. While fasting from food is appropriate for many, it is not for someone who has struggled with an eating disorder. Linda told me that instead of starving myself, I needed to nourish myself on God's love. She then offered me what I now term the Twenty-Minute Worship Challenge: "Rather than fasting, I want you to offer twenty minutes of worship to the Lord daily. Spend this time just praising the Holy One for His love and goodness, and I believe you will begin to experience God's love in a deeper way."

That challenge changed my life! The first morning I wondered where I would start and how I would fill up twenty minutes. I turned on some worship music to help prompt my thoughts and began praising God through the alphabet:

Lord, I praise you because your love is awesome.

I praise you because your love is boundless.

I praise you that your love is compassionate.

I praise you because your love is delightful . . .

To my surprise, time flew by, and I continued praising and worshiping the Lord for much longer than twenty minutes. The next morning, I couldn't wait to get up and begin again. As I exalted the Lord for His love, something new began to happen in me. For the first time in my life, I began feeling the love of God. My spirit resonated in harmony with the Holy Spirit. The more I worshiped, the more the Holy Spirit opened my heart so that I could experience all the love the Father desired to pour into it.

Ruth Myers writes, "Praise increases our faith as we pray."[3] When you and I worship Christ, the Holy Spirit quickens our hearts and infuses us with more faith to be able to comprehend "how wide and long and high and deep is the love of Christ, and to know this love that surpasses knowledge — that [we] may be filled to the measure of all the fullness of God" (Ephesians 3:18-19). Worship becomes a love exchange. The more we express our love and adoration to God, the more His Spirit enables us to experience His love for us.

Christ is honored when we come to worship hungry for His love. Sam Storms suggests that "worship is a feast in which God is the host, the cook, the waiter, and the meal itself. I must come to worship hungry."[4] When we come to the Bread of Life for His love, He receives all the glory for being the only One able to satisfy that hunger.

Are you having trouble feeling and experiencing God's love? Let me offer you the Twenty-Minute Worship Challenge. Try it for at least a month and see if you begin to feel the love of God in new ways. But don't stop with worship. Let worship lead you into the Word of God. There you will find love messages addressed to the most personal needs of your heart. God's Word is His love letter to you.

CONSUME HIS LOVE LETTER

When my children were young, I packed their lunches for school, often tucking little love notes in their lunch boxes. Sometimes I wrote the notes on their napkin; other times I wrote them on small pieces of paper. Either way, my notes assured my children that their mama loved and cherished them.

God's Word does the same for us. When we read His love letter daily, He can assure us of His unfailing affection. As we choose to feed our hearts on the Word of God, the Holy Spirit nourishes us with His love.

Often in the predawn hours of the morning, I lie in bed and ask the Holy One to fill me up with His love. I pray, "Oh, Lord, I know in my head you love me, but I want to experience it in my heart." I find it helps to personalize Scripture, so I plead, "Satisfy me this morning with your unfailing love, Lord" (based on Psalm 90:14). I whisper, "Lord, help me to remember as I go through this day that you take great delight in me, rejoice over me with singing, and promise to quiet my heart with your love" (based on Zephaniah 3:17). I thank Him that because of His great love I am not consumed by the chaos of life, for His compassions never fail. They are new every morning (based on Lamentations 3:22-23). As I personalize these verses and meditate on them, they nourish my need to feel loved.

But simply reading Scripture didn't seem enough for me when I most needed to feel God's love. Therefore, I disciplined myself to meditate and memorize certain passages so my mind had a place to camp out whenever I was feeling unloved. I often used my walking time to memorize. Whenever I need to feel loved, I recall some verses that assure me that I am God's beloved.

I asked several friends how they feed their minds on the love messages in God's Word and have included their responses below. Why not choose one idea and try it over the next week? You'll be amazed at the big difference you'll feel with just a little effort.

- During the painful months following her divorce, Sara needed constant reminders of God's deep love for her. She wrote out meaningful Scripture verses, personalizing each one so they became love notes from God to her. She keeps these love notes on top of her desk at work. Whenever she starts feeling unloved or rejected, she reaches for a card to center her mind once again on God's unfailing love.

- Jill installed a program on her computer that feeds her verses in the form of screen savers that remind her of God's love. These encouraging verses float across her computer screen throughout her day at work. Not only do these passages of Scripture feed her mind with love messages, but they also create opportunities for her to share God's love with fellow employees.

- Janet buys artwork with Scriptures about God's love and hangs it throughout her home. No matter what room she is in, she sees reminders of God's love for her.

- A busy mom of three young children, Eileen memorizes Scripture verses using index cards taped to her mirror or car dashboard. The Holy Spirit brings the verses back to her memory as she is rocking a baby or fixing lunches or rushing her little ones off to school. Eileen is learning the power of praying those Scriptures over her young children, asking the Holy Spirit to awaken their hearts to know Christ's love.

As we feed our minds on His Word, the Holy Spirit pours assurance of God's love into our hearts. But God also uses other believers to allow us to feel His love.

TASTE HIS LOVE THROUGH OTHERS

Though God is the only One who can satisfy our deepest hunger for love, He chooses to use other people to help us experience His love. These people become "Jesus with skin on" for us. Just as there is an interdependent relationship in the Godhead between Father, Son, and Holy Spirit, so we need the fellowship and direction of others within the body of Christ. God created and wired us with this need (see Genesis 2:18). Paul recognized this and invited other believers to join him in his struggle by praying for him (see Romans 15:30). Living out the Christian life is a struggle at times, and we need others to pray for us, walk alongside us, encourage us, and cry with us. In this way, Jesus' love flows through their hearts to ours.

Many married women depend solely on their husbands for love and support. Often this places too large a burden on their husbands' shoulders. Whether single or married, women need other women. Godly husbands are wise to recognize and encourage this.

During some of the most difficult experiences of my life, God has allowed me to feel His love through others. The year I struggled with breast cancer and had to face a double mastectomy and multiple surgeries, Steve loved and cherished my new body. He continually reassured me of his love and devotion and even accompanied me to doctor's appointments. He also encouraged me to process some of the feelings brought on by breast cancer with Linda, my mentor. She, along with other girlfriends, faithfully loved me, cried with me, and cheered me on through all the changes my body encountered.

Linda also had the wisdom to recognize that my insatiable need for love was symptomatic of a deeper problem, and she suggested that I start meeting with a godly, professional counselor she knew. While I was in counseling, the missing piece to some of my deep insecurities surfaced. I began to remember episodes of childhood sexual abuse that I had not wanted to face or talk about with anyone. (Please be aware that memories of sexual abuse don't just randomly surface, and good counselors don't work to "dig stuff up." Memories of sexual abuse always come in concert with other symptoms and as the missing piece to an otherwise incomplete puzzle.) Steve and Linda's love and acceptance during this dark time gave me a tangible picture of how God viewed me. With their help and my counselor's love and encouragement, I was able to move beyond the memories to complete healing, which ultimately comes through Jesus Christ..

Godly friends and mentors love us when we radiate joy and when sorrow floods our souls. They faithfully cheer us on, encouraging us to draw closer to the Lord. They pray for us, provide accountability, and push us to become all that God desires us to be in Him. Often when I describe how being mentored has helped me, other women say, "Oh, I need that." If this is your desire, ask God to bring a godly mentor into your life, and be patient. He will answer in His time. In the meantime, consider how you might feed those around you with the love Christ offers. Ask God to lay someone on your heart, and then come alongside her. Allow her to experience God's love through you.

While we can taste Christ's love through others, their love can never be a match to His. Jesus invites us to remember and relish what He did out of love.

RELISH HIS LOVE AT THE
COMMUNION TABLE

When Jesus broke the little boy's bread on the grassy hillside, He gave us a picture of His own body being broken for us. The Bread of Life would be broken on the cross so that any who hungered would be able to receive His love. During the Last Supper, Christ took bread and broke it, saying, "Take and eat; this is my body." As He lifted the cup of wine, He said, "Drink from it, all of you. This is my blood of the covenant, which is poured out for many for the forgiveness of sins" (Matthew 26:26-28).

Jesus' death is the single greatest demonstration of love ever offered because "greater love has no one than this, that he lay down his life for his friends" (John 15:13). "But God demonstrates his own love for us in this: While we were still sinners, Christ died for us" (Romans 5:8). This is why He invites us to remember what His love cost Him every time we take Communion.

Sadly, many of us have lost the wonder that captured our hearts when we first took Communion, and it has instead become a spiritual ritual. As a result, we aren't fully engaged when we take Communion, and we miss the opportunity to enjoy God's love for us personally through the bread and the cup. If you have lost some of the wonder you once felt about Christ's love and the Cross, ask the Holy Spirit to kindle a renewed desire within you. Ask Him to stir up in you the divine ache you once felt to know Him more. You might pray as David did: "Create in me a pure heart, O God, and renew a steadfast spirit within me" (Psalm 51:10).

If you long to taste God's satisfying and perfect love for you, commit to making Communion a special time between you and the Lover of your soul. Prepare for Communion by asking the Holy Spirit to soften your heart, enabling you to recapture the wonder. Take some time to reflect quietly on the crucifixion. If you've seen the movie *The Passion*, allow your mind to rehearse some of the scenes. Before you lift the bread to your mouth, pause and praise Jesus for His bruised and broken body, evidence of His love for you. Engage your mind and heart as you lift the cup and drink. Thank Him for the agony He endured for you. Don't allow your mind to wander. Respond to the love initiated by the Lamb of God by expressing your love for Him in worship.

The better you understand His work on the cross, the more you will experience the depth of His love for you.

THE MYSTERY OF SATISFIED HUNGER

Come to the Bread of Life hungry for His love. Don't just nibble. Come to Jesus daily, moment by moment, to have your need for love satisfied.

Try the Twenty-Minute Worship Challenge, feasting on His love. Consume His love messages. Ask Him to show His love to you through others. Allow Him to multiply His love in you, giving you a vision for how you can feed others. Pause the next time you come to the Communion table and relish His love. My prayer is that you will come to Him daily, experience His love as completely satisfying, and return again and again to His never-ending supply.

Recently my husband and I were interviewed by a group of young couples who wanted to ask us about our spiritual walks and marriage. When asked if he protects me from the stress of ministry, Steve replied, "Protect her? No way! I lean on her. She has discovered how to have her needs met by the Lord in a way I am still learning."

Wow! When Steve spoke those words, I realized that he no longer felt I was high maintenance. I am now learning to love my husband from the overflow of a full cup. The cracks that had prevented me from feeling loved have been healed. As I keep returning to the Bread of Life to have my soul filled, He awakens more hunger for Him. This is the mystery of being satisfied. My heart now cries out with David, "Because your love is better than life, . . . my soul will be satisfied as with the richest of foods; with singing lips my mouth will praise you" (Psalm 63:3,5).

> *Lord, I come to You as the Bread of Life. I have tasted of Your love, but I long to experience that love more fully. Help me to come to You daily with my hunger. I worship You as the only One who can completely satisfy the deepest longings of my heart.*

CHAPTER 4

HEY, I NEED A LITTLE DIRECTION HERE!

"I am the light of the world."
JOHN 8:12

I recently saw an illustration on the cover of *Discipleship Journal* that caught my eye. Pictured was a game spinner with the following choices in boxes: Go, Stay, Yes, No, Pray More, Spin Again.[1] I grabbed the magazine, thinking, *Wouldn't it be great if we could just spin a spinner to discover God's will?* As much as we might wish otherwise, the process of discovering God's will is rarely so cut and dried.

How do we discern God's will, particularly when trying to answer questions such as these?

- Should I buy or rent a home?
- Should I have the surgery or go a less invasive route?
- Should we get married?
- Should I go back to work now that the kids are older?
- Should I work full-time or part-time?
- Should we start a family?
- Should my children attend public or private school, or should we homeschool them?

- Should I entertain a career change?
- Should I accept the job offer, even if it means moving my family?
- Should I attend a different church?

How do we decide? How do we know what's best, particularly when we have several viable options? How do we know *which* option is the *right* option?

As I write this chapter, my husband and I are seeking God's direction for our lives. Steve resigned from his ministry position many months ago, and although we have considered many opportunities, we are still unsure of what God wants us to do next. It is my prayer that the lessons we have been learning will benefit you and shed some light on how to discern God's leading in your own life.

In times like these, it's good to know we have a guide. Jesus said, "I am the light of the world. Whoever follows me will never walk in darkness, but will have the light of life" (John 8:12). In order to understand Jesus' claim to be the light of the world and the impact it can have on our decision making, we need to visit the Jewish celebration of the Feast of Tabernacles.

TIME TO CELEBRATE

Every year in late summer or early fall, the Israelites traveled to Jerusalem for seven days of feasting, which culminated in a grand celebration held in the temple. God ordained this holiday so that the Jews would never forget what He had done for them during their forty years in the wilderness (see Leviticus 23:39-43).

During their wilderness wanderings, the Israelites had often camped in desolate places — sites far from shade or the comfort of an oasis. But their location didn't really matter because "by day the LORD went ahead of them in a pillar of cloud to guide them on their way and by night in a pillar of fire to give them light, so that they could travel by day or night" (Exodus

13:21). If the pillar moved, they broke camp and followed, no matter how comfortable the campsite, how short the stay, or how weary the people.

On the last day of the Feast of Tabernacles, the Day of the Great Hosanna, a specially appointed priest poured water from a golden pitcher over a rock, symbolizing God's divine provision of water that gushed from the rock in the wilderness (see Numbers 20:8-11). While the priest poured, trumpets blasted and choirs formed a procession, singing praises to the Holy One of Israel. Crowds marched, waving palm branches and chanting Psalms 113–118, which ends with these words:

> "The LORD is God,
>   and he has made his light shine upon us.
> With boughs in hand, join in the festal procession
>   up to the horns of the altar. . . .
> Give thanks to the LORD, for he is good;
>   his love endures forever." (Psalm 118:27,29)

Passionate praise filled the temple as the worshipers celebrated the goodness of the Lord.

Jesus and His disciples were in Jerusalem to participate in this festive remembrance. On the last day of the feast following the exuberance of the celebrative worship, Jesus stood and spoke with the voice of authority, declaring, "I am the light of the world." To the Jews His meaning was undeniably clear: "I am the light that led you through the wilderness." In that one defining moment, I suspect that the Jewish leaders and crowds were stunned to silence and that all celebration ceased. With this claim, Jesus, the son of a humble carpenter, was declaring Himself to be God. The Jews knew that the light of blazing fire that had guided their ancestors through the wilderness had been God Himself. By calling Himself the light of the world, Jesus was claiming that He was God and would guide them just as He had done in the wilderness. He was promising to illumine every path they were to follow. And, as incredible as it sounds, He promises to give the same direction to you and me!

I don't know about you, but that gives me great comfort because in the midst of life's choices, I need a guide. I can't just randomly move through life without knowing why I'm here, what I'm doing, or where I'm going. I need to know that there is purpose and meaning in my existence. I need a sense of destiny. Jesus is the one who illumines my destiny and direction, and He can illumine yours.

HOW GOD GUIDES

David wrote,

> "The law of the LORD is perfect,
> > reviving the soul.
> The statutes of the LORD are trustworthy,
> > making wise the simple. . . .
> The commands of the LORD are radiant,
> > giving light to the eyes." (Psalm 19:7-8)

The first place we should turn when trying to discover God's will is to *the Word of God* because in it, God gives us specific commands as well as principles for how He wants us to live.

For example, suppose you have been dating a man for a few months and are in love with him. He has many of the qualities you have always longed for in a mate, but he's not a follower of Jesus Christ. Then one night at dinner he pops the question, "Will you marry me?" What should you do? Open the Word. Does God have anything to say about the kind of person a Christian should marry? Yes. According to 2 Corinthians 6:14, we are not to be "yoked together with unbelievers" (and marriage would put you in a binding yoke). The Bible illumines God's will about many life choices, such as:

- Whether to forgive (Ephesians 4:32)
- Whether to remain sexually pure (Colossians 3:5)
- Whether to remain faithful in marriage (Exodus 20:14)
- Whether to try out a "new religion" (Exodus 20:3-4)

While God's Word clearly addresses some life choices, it doesn't specifically address most of our choices. Yet even in these gray areas, God's Word can offer principles that can guide us. For example, 1 Corinthians 6:12 offers this wise counsel: "'Everything is permissible for me' — but not everything is beneficial." This principle can be useful when determining whether you participate in some action, such as viewing a particular movie or reading a particular book. Ephesians 6:4 presents a principle that can be helpful when deciding how to discipline a child. It wisely instructs that as parents we are not to "exasperate" our children by laying unrealistic or harsh demands on them, but rather we are to nurture them in gentle discipline and instruct them in God's ways.

In addition to offering guidance through His Word, God also offers direction through *the inner promptings of His Holy Spirit.* Jesus promised that He would give us the Holy Spirit to indwell and lead us. We see evidence that He fulfilled this promise in the book of Acts when some believers met for prayer, presumably to decide about further ministry involvement. We learn that "while they were worshiping the Lord and fasting, the Holy Spirit said, 'Set apart for me Barnabas and Saul for the work to which I have called them'" (13:2). The Holy Spirit still indwells us and speaks to us today. He is with you and will guide you (see John 16:13).

God also uses wise counselors to help us discern His will. Proverbs 19:20 says, "Listen to advice and accept instruction, and in the end you will be wise." Over and over again, God's Word encourages us to seek the counsel of people who are wise. In the Old Testament book of Ruth, we find that Ruth asked and received the counsel of her wise mother-in-law,

Naomi, regarding decisions about getting a job, pursuing Boaz (the man she married), and getting married (see Ruth 2:2; 3:1-5, 18).

God will provide a light for our path, but we first must be willing to follow it.

SET YOUR HEART TO FOLLOW

As Christians, we have a leader. Jesus' instructions are clear: "Come, follow me" (Matthew 4:19). The Greek word Jesus used here for "follow" is *akoloutheo*, which "expresses union, companionship, going in the same way."[2] In other words, if we are going to follow Jesus, we must bring our will into union with His will. He's the leader; we're the followers. If we want God's guidance, we must set our heart on obeying Him.

A heart set on following Christ is one that inquires and relinquishes. Let's take a closer look at each of these.

A heart that inquires asks for God's guidance. How can we know God's will if we do not ask Him? James instructs that whenever we are not sure what to do, we are to ask for God's wisdom (see 1:5). God never runs out of wisdom, no matter how challenging our situation (see Romans 11:33-36).

On rare occasions God gives wisdom for a situation all at once, but more often He unfolds His wisdom one small portion at a time as we continue to ask for His guidance. I believe this pattern demonstrates His desire for us to keep coming to Him. If God gave all the wisdom we needed to make a decision the moment we asked Him for it, our inclination might be to screech into His throne room, grab a quick piece of advice, and then race out, rather than lingering in His presence and feasting on the depths of His wisdom. God delights in the one who dwells in His presence, continually seeking His counsel.

King David exemplified this kind of dependence on God for guidance and wisdom. Scripture tells us that he "inquired of the LORD" (2 Samuel 2:1). I love this verse. It speaks of the pattern of David's life. God honored

David by calling him a man after his own heart who would do His will completely (see Acts 13:22).

How often have we tried to solve life's problems through our own efforts, rushing ahead with our own plans without seeking the counsel of the One who is to light our way? Instead, we are to draw near to God and ask Him, "What would You have me do?" Author Alan Redpath writes, "If you are not sure, get alone somewhere with God until every other voice is silent and all human opinions are shut out, and learn to look to the Lord."[3]

I know a retired couple who inquires of God every day for their "marching orders." They ask God how He wants them to spend their day, and then they follow what they believe He is leading them to do, whether it is to share Christ with a neighbor, volunteer at a homeless shelter, assist a widow with home repairs, or serve at church. Whether we are trying to decide how to spend our day or are wrestling with a major decision or problem, we can ask God for guidance. Only then can we become women after God's heart who, like David, inquire of the Lord and then follow His direction.

A heart that relinquishes lets go of anything that stands in the way of following God's will. When our daughter Stefanie was ten, she wanted to be baptized. When I asked her what she thought it meant to be baptized, she started spouting the typical answer: "It means I want to follow Jesus. It means I will go under the water like Jesus was buried and then come up out of the water like Jesus came up out of the grave." Then she paused, and as I sat silently waiting, she blurted out, "And it means I can't talk back to you anymore!" Stefanie understood what it means to follow Jesus. For her, following Jesus meant she had to stop speaking disrespectfully to her parents. At the time, I nodded soberly and told her she was exactly right. Later I told Steve, "Don't mess with her theology!"

It costs something to be a disciple. Jesus said, "If anyone would come after me, he must deny himself and take up his cross daily and follow me" (Luke 9:23). If we want to follow God, we need to let go of anything that displeases Him or prevents us from following Him. To relinquish something means to let go of it. Following Jesus might mean letting go of a displeasing attitude or sinful behavior, or it might mean releasing something good, perhaps a gift from God that He wants us to place back in His hands. I believe this is what God asked me to do when He led us to move to California.

When we lived in upstate New York, we built a beautiful home on a three-quarter-acre lot complete with woods and a stream in the backyard. I remember the excitement of building and the joy of decorating our new home. Finally, after years of living in a tiny home with four kids, I would be able to enjoy entertaining in a spacious home. I loved that home. But I also knew the house had been a gift from the Lord and was to be used to honor Him. Two and a half years after we built that house, God led us to California, and I had to relinquish it.

Are you willing to relinquish whatever might stand in your way of following God's light? Your agenda? Your dreams? Your possessions? Your children's future? If anything stands in your way, God invites you to let go and place it in His hands.

The psalmist paints a picture that I think sums up what it means to have a heart set on following God. He wrote, "As the eyes of slaves look to the hand of their master, as the eyes of a maid look to the hand of her mistress, so our eyes look to the LORD our God" (123:2). The servant of an Eastern woman was trained to keep her eyes fixed on her mistress. At the slightest sign or gesture, the servant moved into obedient service to the master.[4] In a similar way we are to fix our eyes on God, looking for the slightest movement that may indicate what He wants us to do so that we can respond with obedience.

But even after we have set our heart on following God, how can we be sure that what we are hearing comes from Him, and how do we discern what He is saying?

TAKE PERSONAL INVENTORY

Steve and I have learned the benefit of asking probing questions when we are trying to hear God's voice. The following questions can be used to try to discern God's leading. The questions are meant to assist you as you spend time in God's presence seeking His will. They are not meant to be a quick list to run down and check off; rather, they are meant to encourage you to linger and listen patiently for God to speak. Too often when we don't find God's direction in the first five minutes, we give up, assuming He has no opinion. But when the prophet Jeremiah asked God where the Israelites should go and what they should do, God waited ten days to answer (see Jeremiah 42:3,7).

Remember, God may light the entire path all at once, or He may light the path one tiny step at a time. David wrote, "Your word is a lamp to my feet and a light for my path" (Psalm 119:105). This verse gives a picture of God shedding just enough light on the path to take the next step. Having said that, let's look at each of these questions.

1. *What Does God Seem to Be Saying in His Word?* One of the ways God speaks is through His Word, so when seeking to determine His will, we can watch for patterns in what He seems to be telling us through the Bible. For example, several years ago I felt very concerned about an attitude one of my children was displaying. Knowing how difficult it would be to broach this subject with a teenager, I went first to the Lord for counsel on what to say to my child. I asked God to show me from His Word what to say. Over the next few days I wrote down all the verses that seemed to jump off the page at me during my daily Bible reading. These are some of the verses I recorded (all from Proverbs):

> When words are many, sin is not absent, but he who holds his tongue is wise. (10:19)

The lips of the righteous nourish many. (10:21)

But a man of understanding holds his tongue. (11:12)

Reckless words pierce like a sword, but the tongue of the wise brings healing. (12:18)

The wise woman builds her house, but with her own hands the foolish one tears hers down. (14:1)

When I reviewed the verses I had written down, I noticed a pattern that surprised me. I felt God was asking me not to say anything to my daughter about her attitude. His answer didn't make sense to me at the time because I felt anxious to "fix" this attitude in my teen. Still, I decided to follow the guidance He had given me.

Several weeks later, this child apologized for the very attitude I had felt concerned about and also confided in me about the anxiety driving the attitude. If I had rushed ahead instead of seeking God's guidance, my teenager's heart would likely have been closed. By heeding the counsel I found in God's Word, I had a delightful teaching moment with an openhearted child.

2. What Does the Holy Spirit Seem to Be Prompting Me to Do?

Scripture clearly teaches that the Holy Spirit offers guidance to believers:

"When he, the Spirit of truth, comes, he will guide you into all truth." (John 16:13)

While they were worshiping the Lord and fasting, the Holy Spirit said, "Set apart for me Barnabas and Saul for the work to which I have called them." (Acts 13:2)

So when seeking guidance, we also need to listen for the voice of the Holy Spirit. What does He seem to be saying about the matter?

To discern this, you might ask God what He wants you to do and then sit in silence for a while, listening for Him to speak to you. What thoughts or impressions come to mind? As you continue to pray about the decision, listen for the voice of the Spirit. What does He seem to be saying?

When our son JJ was thirteen, he complained of a stomachache and spent an entire day vomiting. By the end of the day he felt fine and even ate a piece of strawberry pie. But early the next morning he came into our bedroom, again complaining of stomach pain. He was no longer vomiting, so I sent him back to bed. It was Sunday, and I decided to allow him to stay home from church and rest, thinking he'd be fine by the next morning in time for school.

Meanwhile, I went downstairs to spend some quiet time with the Lord. While I was on my knees asking God for wisdom about what to do for our son, the thought came to me that JJ had something worse than the flu. My initial thought was *That must be my fear talking*, but then I asked the Lord to show me if it was the Holy Spirit speaking. Again I felt an urgent prompting to get my son to the doctor. The thought simply wouldn't go away. Thankfully, I listened. As it turned out, JJ's appendix had ruptured. If I had waited much longer, I could have lost my son.

When answering the question, What does the Holy Spirit seem to be saying? keep in mind two principles that can guide us in discerning whether what we are "hearing" is truly from God or if it's from another source, such as our own thoughts or desires.

a. *The Holy Spirit's leading will never contradict Scripture. If the message we hear encourages us to do something that Scripture forbids, it's a sure sign that the message is not from God.*

b. The Holy Spirit's voice is persistent. If we keep getting the same message over a period of time, it could very well be from God.

If you have evaluated the message using these principles and are still unsure, consider doing what Gideon did: Put out a fleece. Gideon was an Old Testament judge who asked the Lord's guidance before going to war against the Midianites and Amalekites. Gideon wanted to be sure the Lord had called him to fight this battle, so he laid out a wool fleece before the Lord. He asked Him to drench with dew only the fleece — not the ground around the fleece — if God was with them. The next morning when Gideon went out to check the fleece, it was wet but the ground was dry. Still, Gideon wanted to be sure this wasn't just an accident, so he laid out the wool fleece once again, this time asking that the fleece would be dry but the ground around it wet. Again the Lord confirmed that He would be with them in battle (see Judges 6:36-40). When we need reassurance that we have heard the Holy Spirit correctly, God allows us to put out a fleece.

Our daughter Stefanie learned this last summer. She was trying to discern God's will regarding whether she should go on a mission trip to Belize. She initially believed that God was leading her to go on the trip, but when the funds didn't come in, she began to question that leading. She decided to ask the Lord for a clear sign that He wanted her to go. That night she knelt by her bed and prayed, "Lord, there are only two weeks left till I'm supposed to leave. If you want me to go, would you bring in one thousand dollars in two weeks? I'm going to trust you and plan to go unless you show me otherwise." God answered her bold request. The one thousand dollars arrived in the next two weeks, confirming Stef's belief that it was God's will for her to go.

3. *Which Option Brings God the Most Glory?* God created us to bring Him glory, and Paul instructs that whatever we do, we are

to do it for God's glory (see 1 Corinthians 10:31). When we bring God glory, we allow Jesus, the light of the world, to brilliantly radiate through our lives so that others can see Him more clearly. Any activity or decision that clouds His reflection in us doesn't bring God glory. Pastor and author John Piper says it this way:

> Jesus created us in his image so that we would image forth his glory in the world. We were made to be prisms refracting the light of God's glory into all of life. Why God should want to give us a share in shining with his glory is a great mystery. Call it grace or mercy or love — it is an unspeakable wonder. Once we were not. Then we existed for the glory of God![5]

Nina asked herself this question when considering whether or not to divorce her husband. Although God hates divorce (see Malachi 2:16), one could argue that Nina had biblical grounds for divorce because her husband had been sexually unfaithful to her not just once but several times (see Matthew 19:9). But after prayerfully considering which decision would most reflect Christ, Nina chose to remain in her marriage. She forgave her husband and entered counseling with him. Through her decision, God has received glory and honor. Even the psychologist who counseled them, although not a Christian, calls the healing that has taken place a miracle.

Tammy and Ben also asked this question when Ben was offered a big promotion at work. While the promotion meant more income, it also meant more hours and traveling time. After prayerfully considering which course would bring God the most glory, Ben decided to turn down the promotion, realizing it would take too much time away from his wife and three children. Ben decided Christ's image would be most glorified in him if he faithfully kept his priorities straight.

Even children are able to understand this concept. When our kids were in elementary school, I prayed over them every morning and reminded them to shine for Jesus in school. They understood that they had the opportunity every day to reflect Christ in school. How they chose to reflect Him would either make Him look bigger or smaller in their lives.

4. *What Is the Best Use of My Resources?* When trying to discern God's will, we sometimes need to stop and consider how our resources — our talent, money, time, skills, and energy — will best be used for God's purposes and kingdom. Jesus taught us in the parable of the talents how important it is for us to wisely invest the resources He's given us (see Matthew 25:14-30).

Bri-Anne and Tim used this question to help them determine whether to relocate. They had grown tired of the frenetic and fast-paced lifestyle they were living and had begun to question whether living in California was the best option for their young family. They prayed about this decision for a year, asking God for guidance about a move. As they considered options for relocating, they discovered that the cost of living was considerably less in the Midwest and determined that the best use of their resources would be to move there.

Another family used this question when trying to decide whether to keep their children in a private school that was a half-hour drive away. Because all of their kids were involved in sports and music activities, the family's schedule was hectic and chaotic, draining their energy, gas money, and family time. After considering the options, this family decided a better use of their resources would be a school closer to home. As a result, neither parents nor kids are as exhausted and frazzled.

5. *What Are My Mentors Saying?* When grappling with a difficult decision, ask for godly counsel. The Bible tells us, "Listen to advice

and accept instruction, and in the end you will be wise" (Proverbs 19:20). This does not mean blindly accepting someone's counsel. Be sure to pray about her advice and check to see whether it squares with Scripture.

This question helped our friends Gail and John as they tried to discern God's will regarding several job opportunities John had been given. The couple met with the leaders of their church and told them about every job option. The church board knew both Gail and John well; they knew their gifts, strengths, and weaknesses. After John finished presenting each opportunity, he asked, "Which position best fits the gifts and abilities God has given me?" Together with the church board members, John and Gail were able to reach a decision.

TAKE A LEAP!

In closing, I need to point out that God does not always clear away our ambivalence. Sometimes when we think God is asking us to do something, we have to take a leap of faith, even though all the circumstances may not line up. Faith says that if God is leading us, He will help us, even when we can't see how it will all work out.

The writer of Hebrews tells us that faith is "being sure of what we hope for and certain of what we do not see" (11:1). He goes on in chapter 11 to illustrate faith with the stories of men and women who dared to believe God for things they couldn't see and who acted in obedience to His call when they could not understand. Let these stories encourage you:

- When God told Noah to build the ark, Noah did — even though it had never rained a drop before this time. Noah believed God even when he couldn't see the outcome (see verse 7).

- By faith Abraham left the land he was familiar with and moved to the land of promise (see verse 8). Abraham also trusted God for the child promised, even though he and Sarah were long past childbearing years and Sarah was infertile (see verse 11).

- By faith Moses raised his staff over the Red Sea, parting the waters and allowing the Israelites to escape the Egyptians by walking on dry land to the other side (see verse 29).

Keep in mind, however, that following God's guidance does not ensure a "smooth landing." Carol participated in a Bible study in which I taught these principles. At the end of this study, Carol shook her head and said, "Becky, they don't work!" Taken aback, I asked her why she felt this way. She explained that she and her husband had used them when deciding whether to have her mother move in with them. After much prayer, Scripture reflection, and analysis of their financial resources, they felt convinced that God wanted her mother to move in with them, so that's the route they took. With tears filling her eyes, Carol went on to explain that things were not going well. Relationships were strained, tension was high, and Carol felt that she and her husband were at a breaking point. Carol then asked me, "Did I make a mistake?" While it would be impossible for me to know for sure, I told her, "Not necessarily."

For one thing, God's will can change from season to season. Just because God led Carol and her husband to welcome her mom into their home for a season, it doesn't mean that He wants her to live with them for the rest of her life. So it's important to keep asking God if we are still doing what He wants us to do.

For another, God never promises that if we follow His leading, our journey will be smooth. Pastor and author Erwin McManus points out that "the certainty that God has called you and the confidence that He will work His victory out in your life are not guarantees of a safe and secure journey."[6] Following God's will wasn't always problem free for Noah, Moses, and some of the other heroes mentioned in Hebrews 11. Nor was it for Christ. God's perfect will for Him included suffering on the cross.

The key is to set our heart to follow *wherever* He leads. We need to embrace the light He sheds on each particular step and move in that light, trusting that He will reveal the next steps moment by moment.

> "If you have light
> Just for the moment
> In which you find yourself,
> It is enough. . . .
> For you have Him, and
> He is all you need."[7]
> STORMIE OMARTIAN

CHAPTER 5

WHERE DO I HIDE WHEN I'M PETRIFIED?

"I am the good shepherd."

JOHN 10:11

*M*y daughter's journal lay open on her bedroom floor as Steve and I knelt beside her bed, ready to tuck her in and pray with her. I couldn't help but read the first few lines:

> Dear God,
> I always thought nothing bad could ever happen to my family. Now my mom has breast cancer. How could You let this happen? I'm afraid, God.

The anguish and fear behind Keri's words brought fresh tears to my eyes. As I asked her if I could read the rest of her entry for that day, I silently prayed, *Oh, Father, help us. My precious child is so frightened. She's only ten. Please give us words of wisdom to calm her fear.*

I don't remember specifically what we said to our daughter that evening. Frankly, I was trying to keep my own fears from drowning me. The doctor had called late that afternoon with news no woman ever wants to hear: "The biopsy shows malignancy in several areas. We need to schedule you for surgery. The safest option at this point is a double and complete mastectomy." I hung up the phone and tried unsuccessfully to repeat the words to Steve. Fear enveloped me as I looked at my husband's ashen face. I couldn't remember any other time in our marriage when he had looked so afraid.

Together we went downstairs, gathered our four children, and explained what the diagnosis meant as far as surgery. We offered strong words of reassurance about God being in control and guarding us as a family. But the words sounded a bit hollow and passionless. During the family discussion, I held Keri on my lap. I remember wanting to reassure her that I would be fine, that life would go on as usual, and that I would always be there to protect her. But that night as I tucked her in, I felt a strange sense of foreboding. Doubt and anxiety seized my heart as I realized I could not truthfully give her any absolutes about my health. I wanted to be the nurturing mother who would gently reassure, "It's going to be okay," but I couldn't.

The week between the biopsy and the surgery, I had difficulty concentrating. I remembered precious moments when I had nursed my children or enjoyed the embrace of my husband. I wondered about my future and how my illness would impact our lives. A million questions scurried through my mind:

How far had the cancer spread?

What would my body look like after the mastectomy?

How would my husband feel about my body after surgery?

Would I need chemotherapy?

Would I live to finish raising my children?

The words of the Old Testament prophet Habakkuk described my feelings perfectly: "I trembled inside when I heard all this; my lips quivered with fear. My legs gave way beneath me, and I shook in terror" (3:16, NLT).

THE PORTRAIT OF A GOOD SHEPHERD

In the days before my surgery, my mind returned to a picture I had seen hanging in the home of a woman who hosted me when I spoke at her women's retreat just weeks before. The artist had sketched the portrait of a shepherd with a little lamb securely snuggled in his arms. The shepherd's face gazed down with love and concern on the sheep in his arms. As I looked at that picture, my mind immediately went to Jesus' words in John 10:11: "I am the good shepherd."

I longed for the comfort and protection portrayed in that picture. I wanted to nestle securely against Jesus like that little sheep against its shepherd. I wanted to experience God as my Good Shepherd, the One who would protect me from harm. It was the perfect time to return to a beloved passage of Scripture, the Twenty-Third Psalm.

David, the author of this poetic masterpiece, understood the meaning of fear. He lived for many years under the shadow of Saul's threats to take his life. Although at one time Saul had considered David a surrogate son, his affection turned to jealousy after David killed Goliath and the crowds began praising David, saying, "Saul has killed his thousands, and David his ten thousands!" (1 Samuel 18:7, NLT). Saul's jealousy was so intense that he tried several times to kill David. Once while David was playing the harp for Saul, the king threw his spear, trying to pin David to the wall (see 1 Samuel 19:10). Another time Saul sent men to David's bedroom to murder him (see 1 Samuel 19:11-14). Yet another time Saul's own son, Jonathan, helped David escape death by Saul's hand (see 1 Samuel 20). Imagine how it would feel to be hunted by someone intent on murdering you! No wonder so many of the psalms that David wrote address fear.

David also knew a great deal about sheep and shepherding, and in this psalm he describes the protective care of a shepherd over his sheep. He paints the shepherd's portrait with broad brushstrokes, giving us a glimpse into the character of his shepherd. David begins, "The LORD is my shepherd" (verse 1). *Yahweh*, the Hebrew word for Lord, is "the personal, most intimate name

God assigned to Himself."[1] *Rophi*, the Hebrew word for shepherd, describes God as "the God who provides loving care."[2]

With this opening sentence, David gives us his rationale for unshakable confidence even when we are filled with fear. He declares that God is big enough to handle our deepest fears and personal enough to care about our needs. He holds together the oceans and seas. He existed before all things and governs all things. Nothing surprises Him or catches Him off guard. Nothing shakes His confidence or rattles His cage: not cancer, not earthquakes, not terrorist attacks — absolutely nothing. Yahweh is "an unchanging God, an uncaused God, and an ungoverned God."[3]

By calling God *Rophi*, David gives us reason to believe that God deeply loves and cares for us and will protect us, just as a shepherd protects his sheep. Isaiah was speaking prophetically about Christ when he wrote,

> "He tends his flock like a shepherd:
> He gathers the lambs in his arms
> and carries them close to his heart;
> he gently leads those that have young." (40:11)

Our shepherd is completely good, and His every intention toward us, His sheep, is good. He loves us intimately and personally. We belong to Him, and He knows our names (see John 10:14). As we study David's psalm, we realize the Good Shepherd offers us six promises that, if claimed, can help calm our fears regarding our finances, our value, and our fears of change, death, evil, and the future.

HE PROMISES TO PROVIDE FOR YOUR NEEDS

I shall not be in want. (verse 1)

A good shepherd provides for every need of his sheep, and our Good Shepherd is no different. Author Max Lucado wisely points out, "What you have in your shepherd is greater than what you don't have in life."[4]

When hard times hit we might cry, "I don't have enough!" We look at rising house prices, gas costs, college tuition, and food prices, and we panic. We complain that we don't have enough money to pay the bills, time to complete our agendas, or love from our husband or friends. When a crisis hits, whether through illness, job loss, an accident, or some other tragic event, and the bills mount as our income drops, we wonder, *How will I ever pay off my debts?*

God doesn't promise that we won't face financial hardship or even destitution, but He does promise to provide what we need, including what we need financially. While we don't always understand what we need, we can trust that He does and that He will fulfill His promise.

We can see God's faithfulness demonstrated in the life of George Mueller. Mueller was a pastor of great faith who lived in England in the 1800s. During his lifetime, he cared for over ten thousand orphans. He never asked anyone for money to meet the financial needs of the orphanages. Instead, he asked God to provide. For the last sixty-eight years of his ministry, he did not take a salary (gulp!) because he trusted that God would prompt people to send him the money he needed or provide in some other way. "He never took out a loan or went into debt."[5] (Double gulp!) Mueller's life centered on trusting God and simply taking Him at His word.

I first read about George Mueller's life and incredible faith during a time when Steve had taken a huge cut in salary and I was worried about our finances. Mueller's story struck a chord in my heart. Was I satisfied with God and with what He had provided in my life? Instead of worrying that we would not be able to make ends meet, I needed to continually remind myself that if *more* financial blessing was good for us, our loving Shepherd would provide it.

The Good Shepherd wants us to trust Him to give us what we need. Can we echo the faith of George Mueller and say, "If it is good for me, my

Shepherd will give it. I will trust Him and not be afraid"? This is a great statement for us to keep in mind when the fear of hardship knocks on our door.

Our Shepherd promises to provide not only for our financial needs but also for the needs of our soul.

HE PROMISES TO RESTORE YOUR SOUL

> He makes me lie down in green pastures,
>> he leads me beside quiet waters,
>> he restores my soul. (verses 2-3)

As a society we've become addicted to frenetic busyness. Ask the average American woman if she has time to complete everything on her to-do list, and she will look at you cross-eyed. We are a fast-paced, hurried society. Although we whine about not being able to keep up, we never slow down because somehow we confuse busyness with productivity and productivity with worth and value. Life seems great — until something forces us into inactivity. During such times, discouragement and doubt can set in, and our souls can become cast down. In Psalm 42:5 David wrote,

> Why are you cast down, O my soul,
>> and why are you disquieted within me?
> Hope in God. (RSV)

In his book *A Shepherd Looks at Psalm 23*, Phillip Keller points out that when a sheep ends up flat on its back and can't get back up, it's considered "cast down." When this happens, its legs lose circulation and the sheep is helpless to defend itself, becoming easy prey for predators. A good shepherd looks daily for cast down sheep so that he can gently set them back on their feet and rub their legs until circulation has been restored.[6] Our Good Shepherd promises to do something similar for us when we need help getting up on our feet, back on solid emotional footing. He promises to restore our souls.

He did this for me during the slow weeks of recovery following my mastectomy. I could do nothing but lie in bed. All activity came to a screeching halt, and I became depressed and discouraged because I could no longer do the things that brought me fulfillment and made me feel valuable. I received many "Get well" cards, some of which contained the words of Psalm 46:10: "Be still, and know that I am God." But being still was the last thing I felt like doing! Rest wasn't my idea of a good time!

But that's exactly what I needed, and during this time, the Good Shepherd began to restore my soul by teaching me that my worth did not lie in performing. He assured me that if I would just be still and let Him love me, He would set me free from the fear of never being good enough. Instead of building my self-worth on how busy I was, He wanted my self-worth firmly established in the fact that I was His personal lamb.

My friend Bonny needed her soul restored when she walked through the darkness of depression. A former successful and energetic teacher, Bonny had no idea what was wrong when she began to experience fatigue, headaches, stomach problems, and sleeplessness. Bonny had always believed that depression was caused by someone feeling sorry for himself, so she felt devastated when a Christian doctor diagnosed her with severe depression. She felt useless, lethargic, and like a complete failure. Well-meaning Christians made things worse for her by suggesting that if she read her Bible more, prayed more, and examined her life for sin, she would snap out of it. They even told her not to take medication.

Thankfully, Bonny did not listen to her advice-giving friends and instead made an appointment with a Christian psychiatrist. He gently explained to her that depression is an illness that can be brought on by a chemical imbalance or by severe stress. In either case, people don't just snap out of it! He went on to say that if we don't take care of our bodies, we will burn out one way or the other. He prescribed both medication and rest and then calmly assured her, "Bonny, I've never lost a patient yet. If you listen to me and do as I say, you will get through this — but it may take five years!" At first Bonny felt like giving up, and many times through the process of restoring balance she feared she would. But she didn't. Instead she clung to hope that the Shepherd would restore her, reciting Psalm 23 over and over again in her mind.

The Shepherd did restore her body, mind, and soul through people (the psychiatrist, her husband, and others), processes (grieving losses, adapting lifestyle changes, and the permission to feel depressed), medication, and lots of prayer. All were necessary.

Are you feeling discouraged or depressed? The Shepherd delights in helping His sheep who are cast down. He may restore your soul in a moment, or He might use a process. Either way, trust that He will do as He promises.

HE PROMISES TO GUIDE YOU

> He guides me in the paths of righteousness
> for his name's sake. (verse 3)

Moving, whether to a new state, a new country, a new position, or a new season of life, involves change, and change frightens many of us. Guess what? Sheep don't like change either! They are creatures of habit. Sheep naturally go back to the same pastures to graze. But if sheep continue grazing in the same place for too long, they become sickly and weak because the pasture has worn out. "Well worn areas become quickly infested with parasites of all kinds. In a short time a whole flock can thus become infected. . . . So, the wise shepherd keeps them on the move."[7]

The same principle holds true in your life and mine. To ensure that we keep growing in faith and righteousness, the Shepherd sometimes urges us on to new challenges and callings. But He promises to guide us through those transitions, going before us and preparing the way.

In biblical times, shepherds went ahead of the sheep to prepare the grasslands — the "table" — where the sheep would eat. This was a tedious but very important chore. The shepherd uprooted and plucked all poisonous plants so his sheep would not eat something harmful. He did not want his sheep to encounter a situation that he had not foreseen. Nor does our Shepherd, and we can trust that because He is an all-knowing Shepherd, we will never encounter a transition that He did not know about ahead of time.

Are you dealing with a change? A new job? A new child? A relocation for your family? A shift to single life due to divorce or the death of your spouse? A child starting school or leaving for college for the first time? A change of leadership in your church, such as a new pastor or staff member? The Shepherd has already gone ahead and prepared the way for you.

Tanya wondered how she would cope when her husband decided after twenty-four years of marriage that he no longer loved her and wanted a divorce. Tanya wrote me:

> Everything that I had come to rely on, expect, and rest in was shattered. I wondered, Will I ever be loved again? Can I walk into church alone? Can I make that phone call that he would have normally made? How will I live without the physical touch that I so desperately need?
>
> I discovered though, as I started taking tiny steps, that God had prepared the way. For example, when I explained to my boss that I could no longer work for him because I needed full-time employment, he hired me immediately to a full-time position within the same company. This eliminated further job hunting and the stress of adjusting to a new workplace. When I walked

into church alone, I received warm, supportive hugs from friends rather than the judgmental stares I had expected. Gradually, I am learning to put my hand in His, expecting that He will both lead and enable.

Will you, like Tanya, put your hand in His as He leads the way? He promises not only to lead but also to never leave our side, no matter how dark the way becomes.

He Promises to Be Present in Your Dark Valley

> Even though I walk
>> through the valley of the shadow of death,
>
> I will fear no evil,
>> for you are with me. (verse 4)

Most of us fear death to one degree or another. We don't even like to talk about it! But death is a part of life. Sooner or later those we love will die, and so will we. My friend Dale understood this.

Dale died recently, and when I called his precious wife to comfort her and tell her we were praying for her, she shared with me how peacefully he had passed away. She said it was as if Dale had fallen asleep and awakened in the arms of Jesus. Dale had spent a lifetime loving Christ, so death for him was merely stepping from this life into heaven.

For the believer, death is a passing rather than an ending. As Psalm 23 notes, we walk *through* death. We must pass *through* death in order to get to the other side, where there is life. We cannot pass *around* death or *over* death; we must walk *through* it. I find this significant, whether we are talking about physical death, the death of a dream, the death of a marriage, or the death of a vision. When we understand that death is a passageway instead of a destination, it can diminish our fear and offer us comfort. As a shepherd, David knew the only way to lead sheep up to the mountaintop was *through* the valley. On the other side of the valley was new life.

According to Psalm 23, our Shepherd walks beside us through the valley of death. God's Word assures that the Good Shepherd is ever-present and always available to us; He will never abandon us, even in death:

> Neither death nor life, neither angels nor demons, neither the present nor the future, nor any powers . . . will be able to separate us from the love of God that is in Christ Jesus our Lord. (Romans 8:38-39)

> The LORD will not abandon His people. (Psalm 94:14, NASB)

> Never will I leave you; never will I forsake you. (Hebrews 13:5)

Translated from the original Greek, this last verse reads, "I will never, no never leave thee, nor ever forsake thee." Commentator Matthew Henry makes this observation: "Here are no less than five negatives heaped together, to confirm the promise: the true believer shall have the gracious presence of God with him in life, at death, and forever."[8] God will never forsake us — not when facing disease, not when facing divorce, not when facing danger, and not when facing discouragement. Never, no never . . . not even when facing physical death.

My friend Teresa has come close to death many times during her battle with cancer. Each time, God has miraculously spared her life. I have often wondered how she has remained so calm when death hovers so close. In talking with Teresa, I discovered that she decided several years ago to set what she calls a daily plan of living life in the presence of God. Her plan includes conversing with God all day long, turning to Him for wisdom throughout the day, memorizing and studying His Word, and cultivating an awareness of the Holy Spirit's presence.

As a result, Teresa has grown very comfortable with God and feels His presence often. During harsh rounds of chemotherapy or when death hovers imminently, her heart remains calm and steady as she focuses her thoughts on this verse:

> Therefore we do not lose heart. Though outwardly we are wasting away, yet inwardly we are being renewed day by day. For our light and momentary troubles are achieving for us an eternal glory that far outweighs them all. So we fix our eyes not on what is seen, but on what is unseen. For what is seen is temporary, but what is unseen is eternal. (2 Corinthians 4:16-18)

Teresa calmly assures all those around her, "Cancer is only temporary. He will let me come home when He is ready."

The Shepherd promises His presence not only in the dark valleys but also when we come head-to-head with evil.

HE PROMISES YOU COMFORT WHEN YOU FACE EVIL

> Your rod and your staff,
> they comfort me. (verse 4)

When watching the evening news and listening to reports of terrorist attacks, violent crimes, biological warfare, and genocide, we can easily feel surrounded by evil. Often we are tempted to think, *Evil is winning*, which can be truly frightening. How can we experience the Shepherd's comfort in the face of evil?

David was a warrior who had killed wild animals and even a giant.

But he didn't find comfort in his strength and fighting abilities. He found comfort in his Shepherd. He wrote, "Your rod and your staff, they comfort me." What was he referring to?

The rod. A shepherd's rod hung by David's side as his primary weapon of defense. A rod is formed out of a sapling dug from the ground in which "the enlarged base of the sapling where its trunk joins the roots is shaped into a smooth, rounded head of hard wood."[9] The shepherd relied on his rod to keep both himself and his sheep safe from wild animals or other enemies. If a wild animal attacked one of his sheep, the shepherd used his rod to clobber the attacker. One blow could kill an attacking lion or snake.

Keep in mind that David was writing this psalm from the perspective of a sheep. If you were a sheep, imagine how comforting it would be to know your shepherd could wallop any enemy that came at you! According to Philip Keller, we can draw similar comfort from God's Word. He writes:

> Just as for the sheep of David's day, there was comfort and consolation in seeing the rod in the shepherd's skillful hands, so in our day there is great assurance in our hearts as we contemplate the power, veracity and potent authority vested in God's Word. For in fact the Scriptures are His rod.[10]

When we feel defenseless against evil, we too have a weapon — God's Word. Jesus used Scripture when facing evil incarnate, Satan. When Satan tempted Him by saying, "If you are the Son of God, tell these stones to become bread," Jesus answered with Scripture: "It is written: 'Man does not live on bread alone, but on every word that comes from the mouth of God'" (Matthew 4:3-4).

When we are tempted to despair or are cowering in fear over the seeming success of evil, we also can use the comforting words of Scripture to find a safe shelter. Consider, for example, these passages:

God is our refuge and strength,
>	an ever-present help in trouble.
Therefore we will not fear, though the earth give way
>	and the mountains fall into the heart of the sea.
>	(Psalm 46:1-2)

The LORD is my light and my salvation —
>	whom shall I fear?
The LORD is the stronghold of my life —
>	of whom shall I be afraid?
When evil men advance against me
>	to devour my flesh,
when my enemies and my foes attack me,
>	they will stumble and fall.
Though an army besiege me,
>	my heart will not fear. (Psalm 27:1-3)

Your throne, O God, will last for ever and ever;
>	a scepter of justice will be the scepter of your
>	kingdom. (Psalm 45:6)

These verses assure us of God's sovereign control and of His justice that will eventually win over evil.

The staff. The shepherd's staff is a much longer stick than the rod and has a crook on the end. When sheep got too close to the edge of a dangerous cliff, the shepherd could reach out his staff, slip its crook around the sheep's neck, and gently pull the sheep back from danger.

Once again Keller offers us insight into the meaning behind this reference: "Just as the rod of God is emblematic of the Word of God, so the staff of God is symbolic of the Spirit of God."[11] When we are afraid that we or those we love will be drawn in by the lies of the evil one, we can find comfort in remembering that the Holy Spirit dwells within us and can protect us from making wrong choices.

This truth can be very comforting for those of us trying to raise children with a heart for God in a world full of evil. When we fear that our children might make friends with the wrong crowd or experiment with drugs or sex, we can remind ourselves that God is in control and that when the Holy Spirit dwells in the hearts of His children, He can keep them on track. When they veer off the right path, He can lovingly tighten His pull with His staff to bring them back.

God not only promises comfort in this psalm, but even more reassuring, He guarantees our security for all eternity.

HE PROMISES TO HOLD YOUR FUTURE SECURE

> Surely goodness and love will follow me
>   all the days of my life,
> and I will dwell in the house of the LORD
>   forever. (verse 6)

Because we have a Good Shepherd, we don't have to fear the future. No matter what lies ahead for us, God promises that goodness and mercy will always be with us. Jesus declared, "No one can snatch them out of my hand" (John 10:28). His goodness will give us what we need, and His mercy will take care of our sin.

As His sheep, we can calmly and confidently look forward to the future with Him. The future may include changes in our relationships, job, health, church, or place of residence, but we can be assured that the Shepherd will not change. He is our *forever* Shepherd whose love and care for us will remain constant and steady not just today or tomorrow but for all eternity.

Knowing we have such a Shepherd is not enough to quiet our fears, however. We have to move beyond knowing to trusting.

THE ANTIDOTE TO FEAR

Yahweh-Rophi is your personal Shepherd. His character and care are trustworthy. He has promised provision for your needs, restoration for your soul, guidance for your transitions, His presence in your valleys, comfort in your hardships, and security for your future. Trust in His promises, and your fears will dissipate.

How can we let go of fear and claim the Shepherd's promises?

GO TO YOUR WORST FEAR

When we identify our worst fear and the impact it would have on our life if it came true, we can disarm the strength of that fear. I saw this recently with my daughter Keri, who was afraid whenever Steve and I made an international trip together. She feared our plane would crash and she would lose both her parents. Steve and I sat down with her and talked about what would happen if her fear came true. I explained that if Steve and I both died, her older sister would get custody and take care of her. When Keri understood that she would be taken care of by someone who loves her deeply, she relaxed.

What do you fear? Failure? Loss? Tragedy? Terminal illness? Go to your worst fear and ask yourself these questions:

- *Do I have any control over whether this fear will come true?* If you have some measure of control, take action. For instance, I know a woman who fears being raped. She took action to combat this fear by enrolling in a self-defense class. In learning self-defense, she gained a sense of empowerment. Another friend who fears getting cancer studied up on how to guard against cancer through nutrition and changed her eating habits accordingly. While action doesn't offer us complete protection from our fear, it certainly helps increase it.

- *How would my life be impacted if this fear came true?* Would it change your relationship with God? Even if your worst nightmares came true, you would not fall out of the grip of the Shepherd's care. You might go through a period of deep grief, but it could not separate you from God (see Romans 8:38-39).

REMIND YOURSELF OF THE SHEPHERD'S CHARACTER

Your situation has not caught God off guard. He is in control. He is big enough to handle your fear. He is good, and He loves you. If your fear is related to your husband or children, remind yourself that the Shepherd loves and cares for them even more than you do.

When Steve and I lived in Sudan many years ago, our daughter Bethany was a toddler. At eighteen months she contracted a virus that made her extremely ill, and the doctors could not trace the cause. I remember the fear I felt when we put her in the hospital and the doctor told us he did not know what to do for her. That night I knelt by her crib and through many tears visualized myself placing her into the Shepherd's arms. I reminded myself that He is good and that He loves Bethany more than I do, and then I praised Him by faith that He would do what was best. That was perhaps the hardest prayer I have ever prayed. But as soon as I released Bethany into the Shepherd's loving arms, a peace that I cannot explain flooded over me, and I crawled onto the cot next to her crib and slept.

God answered my prayer and healed our daughter: The next day her fever broke. That experience taught me a lesson that I needed for the rest of my parenting years: I must ultimately trust the Good Shepherd with my children's care.

TURN YOUR PANIC TO PRAISE

Perhaps that sounds overly spiritual to you. But really it's not. It is the secret to finding courage. God's Word tells us that He is enthroned in the praises of His people (see Psalm 22:3). When we lift our focus to His character and then praise Him, He honors the tiniest faith and gives us the courage we need in that moment.

As the nurses were wheeling me down the hall to the operating room for my initial six-hour mastectomy, I closed my eyes and prayed, *O Lord, thank You that You are here. Quiet my heart with Your peace.* As I was reflecting on God's character, the Holy Spirit brought Zephaniah 3:17 to my mind:

> The LORD your God is with you,
>> he is mighty to save.
> He will take great delight in you,
>> he will quiet you with his love,
>> he will rejoice over you with singing.

As I went under the anesthesia, I imagined myself snuggled securely in the Good Shepherd's loving arms.

The next time fear threatens to destroy your peace, find shelter in the embrace of the Good Shepherd, who whispers:

Keep On

I know what you are going through.
I know it is not what you expected or planned for.
From the very beginning, I have walked through this with you — and I am with you now.
I am your Good Shepherd
And I will never leave you nor abandon you.
You are never alone!

I know there are times when you are filled with fear, but remember — I will guide you and keep you steady.

I know there are things that cause you worry and anxiety,
but I want you to know that I have promised to provide for you
and all your needs.
When things are unclear; I will be your wisdom . . . when things are
overwhelming,
I will be your strength.
When things are stressful, I will be your rest.

I love you completely!
I am the Shepherd of your Soul.
I want you to trust Me with your future — I will do what is good and
what is best.
You are safe with Me.
Keep On in My Love.[12]

CHAPTER 6

HOW DO I REKINDLE HOPE?

"I am the resurrection and the life."

JOHN 11:25

I lay in bed not wanting to move. The stress of the previous days, months, even years had finally caught up. My normally resilient spirit felt as if it had been snuffed out. One or two losses would have been manageable. But the accumulation of multiple losses had taken a toll on my body, soul, and spirit. I was grieving the loss of my breasts to cancer, the loss of close relationships as a result of our move across the country, and the loss of Steve's job due to slanderous attacks, resulting in a loss of security. I felt encased in a dark tomb of depression, and so I prayed:

> *Holy One,*
> *I need You. My energy is gone, and I feel depressed. Lord,*
> *I'm embarrassed to admit that. You know I've been*
> *clinging, praising, trusting. But I feel dead. Dark clouds*
> *have hemmed me in like grave clothes. I surrender my*
> *grief to You. For the glory of Your name, lift me up out*
> *of the pit of depression and free me from the binding*
> *grave clothes of despair. I place my hope in You.*

Life can feel cruel. The apostle Paul wrote, "We were under great pressure, far beyond our ability to endure, so that we despaired even of life. . . . But this happened that we might not rely on ourselves but on God, who raises the dead" (2 Corinthians 1:8-9). How I praise God that those words are written in the Bible! They promise us that when we feel no hope, when loss after loss drives us into despair, we can depend on the One who has the power to bring life from death. He can rekindle our hope.

Oh, how we need hope. Without hope, we lack the energy and desire to go on living, because hope believes something better is coming. When despair hits, we need hope. Jesus came to win a decisive victory over despair. He claimed, "I am the resurrection and the life" (John 11:25).

Let's take a closer look at the circumstances surrounding this bold statement.

WHEN GOD SEEMS ALOOF

The sounds of weeping could be heard coming from the home of Jesus' close friends Mary and Martha because their brother, Lazarus, had died. His death had snuffed out the hope they had held that he would recover from his illness, and along with the mourners came feelings of despondency. When Lazarus had become sick, Mary and Martha had immediately sent word to Jesus, asking Him to come. When He received the message, Jesus appeared unruffled, unmoved, and definitely unhurried! In fact, He sent them a message assuring them that Lazarus's sickness would *not* end in death — and then intentionally stayed where He was, ministering for two additional days (see John 11:6).

But while Jesus lingered, Lazarus *did* die. From a human perspective, it appeared that Jesus had made a huge error in judgment. As if to add insult to injury, He then told the disciples, "And for your sake I am glad I was not there" (verse 15). Imagine their doubt and confusion. "What's up with this, Lord? First you said Lazarus was not going to die. But — he *did* die! Then you say you're *glad* you were not there? Master, you're not making sense!"

When Jesus finally did arrive, Martha ran immediately to Him and accused Him, saying, "If you had been here, my brother would not have died" (verse 21). "If only" is the campground for our mind when life hurts.

If only God had healed my mom . . .

If only God had spared my business from folding . . .

If only God had protected my child from that drunk driver . . .

If only God had changed my husband's cold heart . . .

When life hurts the most and we feel the most desperate, God sometimes seems far off, aloof, removed from our pain. Such moments rock our world and rip our hearts. We know that God possesses the power to do anything, and yet He appears to stand back and do nothing! In those painful moments, our minds accuse Him: *Where were You, God? Where were You when my baby was born with a debilitating and degenerative disease? Where were You during my husband's terminal illness? Where were You when my reputation was being slandered? Where were You the night my son took his first puff of marijuana?* In life's most painful moments, when our dreams for ourselves and our loved ones die, our faith sometimes crumbles and blows away in the breeze, leaving us with daunting questions of doubt.

In her book *When I Lay My Isaac Down*, author and speaker Carol Kent poignantly describes the horrific despair she felt as her dreams and hopes for her only son were shattered when he was convicted and sentenced to life imprisonment for shooting and killing a man. She writes,

> I wondered why God didn't *do* something to keep my son from taking the life of another man. After all, He performed all of those miracles. . . . Did He choose *not* to intervene in the deadly altercation between Jason Kent and Douglas Miller Jr.?[1]

Why didn't God stop His child Jason Kent from committing murder? We don't know, and we likely won't know until we get to heaven. As much as we might wish otherwise, God never promises to spare us from suffering. He only promises to be with us *in* our suffering.

Often our perceptions of God confine Him to a "God box." We imagine that He exists to please us and protect us from all suffering and evil. This is simply not true. As Larry Crabb points out,

> God is not committed to supporting our ministries, to preventing our divorces, to preserving our health, to straightening out our kids, to providing a livable income, to ending famine, to protecting us from agonizing problems that generate in our souls an experience that feels like death.[2]

But He is committed to loving us faithfully (see Isaiah 54:10), to being with us in suffering (see Isaiah 43:2), and to working our suffering out for our good (see Romans 8:28). In dark moments God whispers, "Will you dare to trust Me?" This is the very same thought that Jesus spoke to Martha: "I am the resurrection and the life. He who believes in me will live, even though he dies; and whoever lives and believes in me will never die. Do you believe this?" (John 11:25-26). In essence, Jesus was saying, "Martha, even though Lazarus died, trust Me. I have a plan in mind. It's different than you imagined, but it's bigger than you could ever hope for."

If Jesus had healed Lazarus, then Mary, Martha, and their neighbors would have missed seeing the greatest miracle of their lives. They wanted Jesus to perform a miracle — the healing of their brother — but He wanted to perform the ultimate miracle. He wanted to bring their dead brother back to life.

When we're faced with circumstances that seem too painful to bear, hope dies and we feel listless . . . dead. In such moments, Jesus invites us, saying, "Come to Me. I am the resurrection and the life. I can restore your hope and give you new dreams that are greater than you ever imagined. Trust Me."

How can Christ, the resurrection and the life, help us rekindle hope? Let's return to the story of Lazarus to see what else it reveals about God's character. In doing so, we'll discover why we can feel safe when we run to Him for help and hope when our suffering seems too much.

HE WEEPS WITH US

While at Lazarus's graveside, Jesus revealed the deeply sensitive side of God's nature. When Jesus first arrived in Bethany, only Martha ran to meet him (see John 11:20). Mary remained in the house, weeping with the mourners. I have often wondered why she did this. After all, she was the one who sat quietly at Jesus' feet, soaking up His every word when He visited for dinner (see Luke 10:39). Maybe she felt frozen in grief. Or perhaps she felt deeply disappointed and hurt by Jesus' late arrival and so didn't want to rush out to meet Him.

In any case, it was only after Martha returned and told Mary that Jesus was asking for her that Mary went to Him. The scene was deeply emotional. She bolted out the door and down the path and fell before her beloved Lord, sobbing at His feet. Jesus was so stirred by her tears that He began weeping Himself. Imagine, "Jesus the Creator of the universe, the eternal *I Am*, so strong, so powerful, so wise, so human, stood there with tears running down His cheeks!"[3] Jesus didn't shed just a tear or two. The original Greek implies that He wept.

In the tragic moments of life when we feel as though we would rather give up than face more pain, we can return to these two words and give ourselves permission to weep and grieve. Our Savior sees, hears, and feels our sorrow and weeps with us. He doesn't stand back aloof or arrogantly instruct us to "stop crying" or "toughen up!" Instead, tears stream down His face on our behalf.

Jess Moody writes,

> Did you ever take a *real* trip down inside the broken heart of a friend? To feel the sob of the soul — the raw, red crucible of emotional agony? To have this become almost as much yours as that of your soul-crushed neighbor? Then, to sit down with him — and silently weep? This is the beginning of compassion.[4]

Jesus takes a "real trip" down into your soul every time you are in deep pain. He comforts you with His tears.

I have seen how comforting this truth can be in the aftermath of devastating loss. Our dear friends and ministry partners, Phil and Donna, called us one night with tragic news. A police officer had arrived at their house a little after midnight to tell them that their twenty-two-year-old son, Daniel, had died in a car accident. No other vehicle was involved. To this day, the cause of his death remains a mystery.

Months after their son's death, I asked Phil how he was doing. I couldn't imagine how was he coping with this tragedy. He talked openly with me, sharing his feelings of loss and sorrow. We cried together. And then Phil handed me the book *When God Weeps*[5] and told me that the knowledge that God was grieving with him was helping him make it from one day to the next.

Jesus weeps over our suffering, and in so doing, He shows us an appropriate response to affliction. God gives us permission to release our pain through tears. As we truly grieve our losses, we take a step toward healing... toward restored hope. So give yourself permission to weep knowing that God weeps with you. He not only *longs* to bring hope back to your life; He *can*. And while He certainly has the power to do so instantly and He sometimes does, He often uses others to help us through the process. After all, He is a God who values community (see Genesis 2:18).

HE VALUES COMMUNITY

As He moved toward Lazarus's tomb, Jesus asked that the stone be taken away (see John 11:39). He prayed, thanking the Father that He had been heard, and then called out in a loud voice of authority, "Lazarus, come out!" (verse 43). Mary, Martha, and the other mourners held their breath. The moment seemed suspended in air. But as they gasped at the audacity of Jesus' command, Lazarus stumbled out of the tomb — the one who had been dead now lived!

Then Jesus turned to Mary and Martha and others in the crowd and asked them to help Lazarus "take off the grave clothes" (verse 44). Jesus had instantly raised Lazarus from the dead, and He could have unwrapped his grave clothes — but He didn't. Instead, He called on those who had witnessed the miracle to help Lazarus. This was not a simple process because Lazarus wasn't wrapped in a single strip of cloth. His arms, legs, head, and chest were wrapped with individual strips of cloth. In order to help him remove his grave clothes, they had to take each limb and unwind the cloth that bound him.

I see a lesson here for those of us whose hope has died. Jesus claims that He can bring us from death to life. He already has brought us from spiritual death to spiritual life. But when it comes to resurrecting our hope, He often uses a process that involves others. He uses our friends and counselors to help us take off our "grave clothes" one piece at a time. They do this by faithfully praying for us, listening to us, and offering us wise counsel, helpful service, and compassionate tears. Their love and support keeps us motivated and moving toward hope.

Although Scripture doesn't tell us that Lazarus removed some of the grave clothes himself, it seems sensible to assume that he did. I believe that if you and I want God to restore our hope, we must help remove our own grave clothes. We must do the work necessary to move beyond despair. This may involve doing the work of forgiveness or the work of changing negative thought patterns. It may involve lifestyle changes, such as slowing down or getting more rest. But if we cooperate with others in the work of taking off our grave clothes, we will be privileged to see God transform our sorrow into joy.

HE BRINGS BEAUTY FROM ASHES

In the midst of Mary and Martha's grief when they had no hope that their brother would get well, Jesus said, "Did I not tell you that if you believed, you would see the glory of God?" (John 11:40). He was telling them to trust Him despite the circumstances.

Jesus' words are for us as well. We need to trust the Father with our suffering and ask Him to show us His glory through it. When God begins to use our pain, it no longer feels pointless.

The apostle Peter writes that we are not to be surprised when we suffer; instead he encourages us to "rejoice that [we] participate in the sufferings of Christ" (1 Peter 4:13). This does not mean that when suffering hits we are to jump up and down, saying, "Yippee! I get to suffer with Christ." Rather, it means that we can rejoice because when we go through suffering, we gain a deeper understanding of the suffering Christ endured on the cross because of His love for us. Just as Jesus offered up His suffering to bring glory to God (see John 17:1-2), so we can offer up our suffering as a sacrifice to be used for God's glory as well. We can bow our heads and pray in unison with Christ, "Not my will, but yours be done" (Luke 22:42). God used Christ's suffering on the cross to redeem the sins of many. If we will dare to believe that God can work through our agony, He will also redeem our suffering. He will bring beauty out of the ashes of our pain.

When the Israelites were building the tabernacle, the place where God would dwell, God instructed them to build an altar on which the priest was to continually burn fragrant incense as a blessing to the Lord (see Exodus 30:1,7-8; 2 Chronicles 29:11). This incense was made through a process that involved crushing flowers. In a similar way, our "soul crushing" becomes a fragrant aroma to God when we present it as a love offering to be used for His glory. This is a sacrifice that God delights to receive. Your request for Him to glorify Himself through your pain is far more powerful than asking God to change your circumstances. As He receives glory from your unthinkable sorrow, your hope will be renewed.

I believe suffering gives God glory when it causes us to move closer to Him and when we become more compassionate as a result of it.

Our Pain Causes Us to Move Closer to Him

When the pressures and trials of life feel unbearable and we run to God as our safe shelter and collapse into His goodness, He is pleased.

Joni Eareckson Tada, author and founder of Joni and Friends, has spent more than thirty years confined to a wheelchair due to a diving accident that left her a quadriplegic. She writes, "Heartache forces us to embrace God out of desperate, urgent need. God is never closer than when your heart is aching."[6] Joni is right. As we draw near to God, He will prove Himself faithful and will hold us steady. As those around us watch us relying on His strength, He receives glory and we find hope.

We Allow Our Suffering to Transform Us into Compassionate Servants with a Broader Ministry

Compassionate people are generally those who have experienced suffering firsthand. They know what it feels like to weep in the night, and as a result they are more willing to grieve with others. This is certainly true of my friend Eileen.

Eileen lost her husband of forty-five years to illness. The weeks and months after his death felt excruciating, and she wondered if she would survive. On those nights when grief would flood over her, Eileen would fill the bathtub, and as she soaked, she would cry till she had no more tears. During those months of intense grieving, Eileen decided to minister to other widows so that God might use her pain. That was over six years ago.

Now when Eileen hears of a woman who has lost her mate, she calls that person — and keeps on calling. At times, she just sits and cries with her; other times, she just listens. She brings meals and writes notes or e-mails of encouragement. Eileen has used her loss to enlarge her heart to have a ministry of compassion to other widows, and as a result God has received glory.

So when despair rolls in like a fog, listen for the voice of God. Often the things He speaks to us in those dark moments are truths we can proclaim loudly and broadly when the darkness has passed. Try to journal every tiny lesson you learn so that you can teach and encourage others in their walk with God.

I did this after I was diagnosed with breast cancer. About a year after my mastectomy, a local television network invited me to speak at a women's health symposium on breast cancer and fear. I accepted the invitation and was able to tell a large audience that having God in my life had been key to overcoming my fears.

Our stories are one of the most powerful tools we possess for encouraging others and for demonstrating the power of God. Will you allow Him to use your pain to help bring healing to the life of another or even to bring someone to faith? Jesus was speaking of His own suffering when He said, "Unless a kernel of wheat falls to the ground and dies, it remains only a single seed. But if it dies, it produces many seeds" (John 12:24). In other words, He was saying, "Though I will die and be buried like a grain of wheat, My death and resurrection will bring forth much fruit."

Although spiritual fruitfulness does not bring back the life of a loved one or restore lost innocence or change the painful consequences of sinful choices, it does assure us that good can be resurrected out of evil, that life can be raised out of death, and that hope can be born out of despair. When we see this fruit, we see evidence of God's faithfulness, which creates within us a new zest for life and a reason to celebrate.

HE REMAINS FAITHFUL

The psalmist Asaph wrote, "I cried out to God for help. . . . When I was in distress . . . my soul refused to be comforted" (Psalm 77:1-2). But in the midst of his despair, Asaph taught himself to remember. He said, "I will remember the deeds of the LORD; yes, I will remember your miracles of long ago" (77:11). Later in the same psalm, we can see that his attitude had changed: "Your ways, O God, are holy. What god is so great as our God? You are the God who performs miracles" (verse 13-14). Asaph's hope was restored because he chose to remember the mighty and good things God had done in the past. His remembering acted as kindling and stoked the embers of his hope when the flames had died.

Do you want to rekindle your hope? Then you too must remember God's faithfulness. He will not withhold what is good for you (see Psalm 84:11). He has a future and a hope especially for you (see Jeremiah 29:11).

During a particularly rough time for Steve, our eighteen-year-old son, JJ, sent his dad the following e-mail:

> Dad, never forget how God has used you in the past.
> Never forget the miracles. His plans for you are good,
> Dad. I love you. You're my hero.

Steve will never forget that e-mail from his son who reminded him that when life stinks and hope is failing, we need to remember the good of the past.

In the midst of your chaos, though you might not feel very hopeful, set aside a few minutes each evening to remember the wonderful moments of the day. Reflect and give thanks for the moments when you felt God's presence, the times you felt the love of a child or husband, or the minutes you enjoyed the beauty of God's creation. If you remember God's faithfulness in your life, your suffering will transform you, and you will emerge with a stronger and more courageous faith.

A MORE RESILIENT FAITH

The apostle Paul wrote, "Suffering produces perseverance; perseverance, character; and character, hope" (Romans 5:3-4). As an equation, it would look like this:

$$\text{Trials} + \text{Tenacity} = \text{Transformation of Character}$$

As our character is transformed, our feelings will follow. We will move from despair to hope, from wanting to give up to the courage to press on. Out of our doubt and despair a more resilient faith can gradually emerge.

As I have looked back over my life, I am overwhelmed by the truth of Jesus' claim, "I am the resurrection and the life." I've found comfort, healing, and hope as I've grieved my losses; taken off my grave clothes with the help of a community of friends, mentors, and counselors; and offered my pain to be used for God's glory. And I have remembered God's faithfulness.

The darkness of despair is gone. Instead, I am free to praise God. His dreams for my life are better than any I could ever imagine. I have seen a glimpse of what He can do as I have told my story, but the greater blessing and joy by far has been the deep intimacy I have found with Him. As I have buried my dreams and embraced His plans for my life, He has resurrected hope. His plans are good. He is unfolding a miracle in my life, and I give Him praise. I thank Him for all that He has allowed in my life, and I celebrate. I want my life to be a symphony of praise because of the hope He has resurrected within me.

> There is no bruised reed that Christ cannot take and restore to glorious beauty. He can take the life crushed by pain or sorrow and make it into a harp whose music shall be all praise.[7]

CHAPTER 7

WHERE CAN I GO TO FEEL AT HOME?

"I am the way."

JOHN 14:6

hen she was single, Julie believed that if she just met and married the right man, she would be happy. She always felt incomplete in some way, and she believed that Mr. Wonderful would fill the void she felt inside. As a wife, she would finally belong; she would feel at home.

But that didn't turn out to be the case.

Three failed marriages later, Julie felt worse than ever. She describes the loneliness she felt as "a throbbing toothache that never went away." Whenever she saw a couple sharing a loving moment — a kiss, an embrace, a touch on the knee, or simply holding hands — it was a painful reminder of what she didn't have. Julie kept telling herself that the problem was that she just hadn't found the right man, so she dove headfirst into another marriage, only to be disappointed once again. A workaholic, husband number four had no time to devote to the marriage, and worse, he continually criticized Julie.

She lost all hope that life would ever be any different, but then she met some Christians who loved her and introduced her to Jesus. As she spent time pursuing a relationship with Him, she felt the satisfying sense of belonging that she had been searching for all those years.

Have you ever felt out of place and disconnected from others, even in a group of Christians? I have. Several years ago I attended a luncheon where I knew only a few women. Though surrounded by many, I felt isolated and lonely. As I listened to the dynamic speaker, I couldn't help but think, *What am I doing here? What do I have in common with these people? I don't fit in here.* I couldn't wait to get back home, a place where people know me and love me for who I am.

HOMESICK FOR GOD

We all long to have a place we can call home, a place where we belong. We were created and designed for community, for knowing and being known. In the beginning of the Bible, we read that "it is *not* good for . . . man to be alone" (Genesis 2:18, emphasis added). While this verse speaks of God creating woman for man and instituting marriage, it also points to the need we have as humans to live in relationship with others. We were created in the image of God Himself (see Genesis 1:26), and for all eternity there has been divine fellowship and community between the Father, the Son, and the Holy Spirit. God created us to be social beings who would crave belonging, particularly belonging to Him.

In our quest for community, we crave the intimacy of feeling connected and finding camaraderie. We yearn for someone with whom we can feel comfortable, accepted, and known. We don't like being alone because that's when we are most likely to feel the pangs of loneliness. In order to avoid this, some of us engage in endless activities and trivial pursuits. Busyness keeps us from having time to think about our longing to belong. But when we stop all the activity, we find we still haven't filled the void in our hearts. Others of us numb our pain through shopping, alcohol, prescription drugs, food, sex, Christian service, work, or our kids. And for a while, we feel better. But once the "fix" wears off, the pain returns because those things don't satisfy the hunger in our souls.

God has crafted each of us with a divine ache, a desire for a safe place of complete love and acceptance. It is a part of our humanness. We can't run from it, hide from it, or escape it. No possession, experience, group, friend, or lover can fill that void because God designed it specifically to be filled with Himself. He alone is the missing piece. We will not be complete until we find our home in Him.

Hudson Taylor, founder of the China Inland Mission, wrote about the heartache he experienced after the death of his wife. With his children far away at boarding school, Hudson felt a deep loneliness and found comfort in Jesus' invitation to find satisfaction in Him. He wrote, "Can Jesus meet my need? Yes, and more than meet it. No matter how sad my bereavement, how far away my loved ones: no matter how helpless I am, how deep are my soul yearnings: Jesus can meet all — all and more than meet."[1]

Only God can satisfy this divine ache in our souls. Jesus came from the heart of the Father, His true home, to a world where people were estranged from Him and each other. On the night before He went to the cross, He gently reassured the disciples gathered in the Upper Room that although He would be leaving them, He would also provide a place of belonging for them.

THE WAY HOME

A sense of dread filled the disciples' hearts as they shared the Passover meal with Jesus. The tension built as Jesus tried to prepare them for what was about to happen. Confusion, doubt, and fear must have plagued their minds as they began to comprehend that the Master was going away.

How could this be? Hadn't Jesus come to establish His kingdom? They had spent the last three years with Him. They had given up their lives for Him. They had believed Him to be the Messiah. Certainly the last three years could not end in defeat! Surely that wasn't the plan! How could He be leaving? What would they do without Him?

In the midst of their confusion, Jesus spoke with gentle reassurance: "Do not let your hearts be troubled. Trust in God; trust also in me" (John 14:1) He went on to say, "In my Father's house are many rooms. . . . I am going there to prepare a place for you. . . . I will come back and take you to be with me that you also may be where I am. You know the way" (verses 2-4).

At this point Thomas cried out the question in everyone else's mind: "Lord, we don't know where you are going, so how can we know the way?" (verse 5). To this Jesus replied, "I am the way" (verse 6).

Jesus' words to the disciples are His words to us as well. Although many of us have been taught that these verses refer to Jesus' return to heaven to prepare an incredible mansion for us to live in for eternity, not all theologians believe this is the only thing Jesus had in mind here. Let me explain.

In his book *The Bush Is Still Burning*, Lloyd John Ogilvie presents another interpretation that is held by some evangelicals. He believes that when Jesus talked about His Father's house and its many rooms, He was referring not only to heaven but also to our true home — God's heart. He explains, "The Father's heart is expansive and inclusive, and has room for all who wish to come."[2] By dying for our sin on the cross, Jesus was able to prepare a place for each of us in God's heart. Because of Jesus' finished work on the cross, we can repent and come home to God.

One of the best illustrations for this picture of repentance can be seen in the familiar story of the prodigal son (see Luke 15:11-32). The story goes like this: A father had two sons. The younger son left home in rebellion against his father's wishes. Like the classic college freshman who leaves home for the first time and ditches his parents' rules, the son spent all his money on wine, women, and wild parties with his new friends. But when the money ran out, so did his friends. What began as independence ended in loneliness. The son "came to his senses," realizing that home was his true place of belonging, and returned to his father in repentance (Luke 15:17).

When we, like the prodigal, try to fill the ache in our hearts with anything less than God, we will be disappointed. Jesus calls us to repent and come back home. He wants us to come back to Him.

Have you been trying to fill a hole in your heart? Do you feel restless or uneasy? Have you thrown yourself into work, hoping to numb your pain or avoid getting to know others intimately? Have you embraced endless activities so that you don't have to think about your life? Have you been chasing Mr. Wonderful? If so, it's time to turn from whatever is keeping you from God and come home.

When we repent, we turn from sin and come to our senses, as the younger son did. We realize that we have been trying to fill our heart with things or people other than with God Himself. We return home by setting our hearts to seek God first.

When we decide to come home to God, Jesus meets us and shows us the way to learn to be at home with God, with ourselves, and with others.

LEARN TO BE AT HOME WITH GOD

Home is meant to be a place where we feel safe. When we feel at home, we don't feel anxious or restless; we don't feel that we have to watch what we say or how we act; we are free to be ourselves. The only place where any of us can feel absolutely safe is in God's presence. That's how David felt. He wrote, "I have stilled and quieted my soul; like a weaned child with its mother, like a weaned child is my soul within me" (Psalm 131:2). This is a description of a child who is content, at ease, and at home in the presence of one who loves him deeply. If you are God's child, that's just how He wants you to feel around Him — at ease and at home.

Because the disciples were used to being with Jesus every day — listening to Him teach, watching Him perform miracles, and fishing, eating, and sleeping with Him — Jesus knew they would need to learn to be aware of His presence when His physical body was no longer with them. As He talked with them in the Upper Room, Jesus promised the disciples that He would provide them with a way to be continually at home with God. Rather than abandoning His followers, Jesus promised to give them the Holy Spirit, the third person of the Trinity, who would not just be *with* them but *in* them (see John 14:16-17). Although the disciples could not imagine how it could possibly be better for Jesus to go away, He told them, "It is for your good that I am going away. Unless I go away, the Counselor will not come to you" (16:7).

The same promise holds true for us. When Jesus lived on earth, He bound Himself to human limitations of body and time. Each disciple had to wait his turn for Jesus' undivided attention. But now, if we have received Christ as our Savior, His Spirit dwells in us. He is continually available to us for whatever we need:

- As our Counselor, the Holy Spirit gives us peace in the midst of feeling upset or confused (see 14:26-27).

- As the Spirit of truth, He corrects our misconceptions and replaces them with reality (see 14:17; 16:8,13). The Holy Spirit brings conviction and correction. He may correct us through our conscience, the Scriptures, or the voice of a friend or conference speaker.

- As our Instructor, He reminds us of Jesus' words and then brings them alive in our spirit (14:26).

- As our Comforter, He continually reassures us of His presence (16:7).

The Holy Spirit is our 24/7 journey mate. If we are God's children, we are never alone. His Spirit lives within us. Nothing can separate us from His presence.

Many Christian women know this truth but have trouble experiencing God's presence, especially in times of loneliness. They wonder if it's even possible. My friend Gail, whom you met in chapter 4, would tell them it is.

Several years ago her husband's job was terminated, and he was offered a job across the country in San Diego. They were used to moving to new places because John had been in the Air Force and they had been missionaries to Southeast Asia. However, having the move sprung on them instead of knowing about it in advance was new to Gail. It just didn't seem fair. They were living near their three adult children, and their first grandchild was soon to be born. She loved her dream home with its forest view. Gail was the women's director at their church and a respected university biology professor, a position that she loved. To make matters worse, her mother died right before they had to move. Angry, Gail railed at God, "How could you ask us to leave at this time and move across the country?"

Gail says,

> When I first arrived in California, I had no friends, no family, no job, no ministry, no reputation, no history — nothing! For days I sat on the couch, depressed and in tears. Why had God allowed this to happen? Although I was very unhappy, I made the decision to be honest with Him about how I felt. One day I told Him, "I know You are supposed to be all that I need, but frankly, You are not enough!" I immediately felt guilty for saying that aloud, but it was truly how I felt at the time.
>
> I had no one to run to but God, so I went to His Word day after long day. As I read huge portions of Scripture, I began to get a renewed view of God. My perspective changed. I saw Him once again as loving. I

realized once again that He was the potter and I was the clay. I ate and drank the Word of God, expecting God to speak to me. As I did, the Holy Spirit broke through my loneliness. Slowly, I began to nestle down, feeling at home in God's presence once again.

Gail did three things that enabled her to access the Holy Spirit and feel at home with God:

- She stopped fighting with Him. Instead, she surrendered to Him her anger about the move.

- She cultivated a sense of God's presence by honestly bringing her feelings to Him in prayer, asking the Holy Spirit to comfort her.

- She also cultivated a sense of His presence by spending time in His Word, expecting Him to speak to her through it.

You too might need to surrender something—perhaps your discomfort about meeting new people, your disappointment over a friendship, or your hurt from feeling rejected. Whatever the case, as you yield more fully to God and spend time praying and reading His Word with the expectation that He will speak to you, you will become more aware of His presence and begin to feel at home with Him.

Christ also shows us the way to be at home with ourselves. This requires the transforming power of the Holy Spirit.

LEARN TO BE AT HOME WITH YOURSELF

A woman who is at home with herself has learned to accept how God created her—physically, emotionally, and spiritually—and what He has allowed in her life. She embraces who she is—her past as well as her present, her weaknesses as well as her strengths, her failures as well as her successes, her sorrows as well as her joys, and her inhibitions as well as her boldness.

Are you able to accept the circumstances and abilities God has given you as gifts from His loving hand? Are you able to say with the psalmist, "LORD, you have assigned me my portion and my cup; you have made my lot secure" (Psalm 16:5)? Are you comfortable with the way He designed you physically and emotionally? Are you able to make peace with His artwork, regarding it as lovely?

This is the attitude King David reflected in the beautiful poetic words of Psalm 139: "For you created my inmost being; you knit me together in my mother's womb. I praise you for I am fearfully and wonderfully made" (13-14). In *Calm My Anxious Heart*, Linda Dillow writes, "In Hebrew, 'inmost being' signified the seat of the desires and longings, the personality. . . . Likewise, when God was forming you, He created not only your body but also your emotional makeup—your personality."[3] In essence, to be at home with yourself means that you are able to say, "I have accepted who I am, and I like who I am becoming."

Our Creator has written the following words to let each of us know how precious we are to Him:

> "I've called your name. You're mine. . . .
> I paid a huge price for you. . . .
> *That's* how much you mean to me!
> *That's* how much I love you!
> I'd sell off the whole world to get you back,
> trade the creation just for you." (Isaiah 43:3-4, MSG)

Paul echoes these thoughts in his letter to the believers in Ephesus: "For we are God's workmanship, created in Christ Jesus to do good works, which God prepared in advance for us to do" (Ephesians 2:10). The Greek word for "workmanship" here could be translated "poem."[4] Your life is a beautiful, poetic masterpiece that God has not finished creating. Are you at peace with the Poet? Have you praised Him for the beauty of His poetic composition? Have you embraced the place God has put you in and the person He's created you to be?

The best way we can learn to be at home with ourselves is by learning to enjoy being alone.[5] If you are thinking, *Why on earth would I want to be by myself?*, please hear me out. We must dare to be alone in the presence of God in order to find our divine center of peace. In solitude, the Holy One breathes into us the courage to face ourselves. In solitude, the Holy Spirit uproots all our preoccupations with self: our self-righteousness, self-hatred, self-doubt, self-negotiations, and self-distortions.

When we are alone, we can listen to our souls. We can ask ourselves, *What am I feeling? Am I bored? Angry? Sad? Depressed? Hopeful? What is behind this feeling? Are my emotions telling me that I need to do something? Grieve something? Forgive someone? Take action about something?*

If we want to become at home with ourselves, it's critical that we become aware of what we are feeling deep inside. Our emotions are what make us feel vibrant — alive. The feelings we own make us unique. Instead of denying them, we need to embrace them, for they will tell us who we really are.

If this sounds scary or suspect to you, you are not alone. Many of us who have grown up in the church don't feel comfortable feeling negative emotions. Somehow we have gotten the idea that being like Jesus requires that we deny or ignore them. This is so wrong! Denying our emotions does not make us like Jesus. After all, He had no difficulty feeling emotion. Scripture tells us He felt anger (see Mark 11:15-17), sorrow (see John 11:35), and joy (see John 15:11).

Use times of solitude to give yourself permission to feel all that rises to the surface: anger, agitation, worry, fear, dread, doubt, and so on. No matter how uncomfortable or even appalled you might feel by your emotions, you must learn to face them so that you can come to terms with them.

Once you have allowed your feelings to surface, take them to the

Holy Spirit, who is our Counselor. In other words, move from a time of introspection to a time of nurturing. As you listen to the voice of the Spirit, He will help you release your hurt, anger, and fear so that you can receive His healing, peace, and courage.

Such times have been a lifeline for me. As I have deliberately chosen to pay attention to what my soul is telling me and then brought that information to my heavenly Father, He has given me insight about what I need to do or be. Sometimes the Spirit nurtures my tired soul, allowing me to simply rest in silence with Him. Other times He invites me to refresh my soul with an activity I enjoy — reading, painting, hiking, or walking the beach. Under His tender care, I have learned to see solitude as precious and critical to my emotional and spiritual well-being. During my alone times I lift my eyes from the desires of my heart to the desires of His heart. As I lift my focus to His plans, He carries me to the place of dreaming. There, the Holy Spirit reveals a glimpse of what I am becoming: calm, confident, courageous, and content. As I realize the transformation that is happening, I find myself not only excited but simply enchanted.

Have you learned to enjoy moments of solitude? Do you use such time to nurture yourself in the presence of the One who loves you more than life itself? If not, why not? Even Jesus modeled the importance of solitude and soul care. He retreated for time alone with the Father and called His disciples to follow His example. He invited, "Come with me by yourselves to a quiet place" (Mark 6:31).

For many women, particularly moms with young children, solitude seems an impossible luxury — something they have for only a few moments a day when the bathroom door can be locked. But all of us can find ways to be alone; we just have to be intentional about it. We have to put time for solitude on our schedules. Those who aren't used to solitude should try to set aside at least three hours a month for self-reflection — and then slowly work up to a full day. If you have young kids, arrange for a babysitter or find another mom with whom you can trade some hours of child care each month.

Even if you have time for solitude, you might struggle with what to do with it. The idea of an entire day of solitude may seem daunting. I've found it helps to have a plan. So when I take a day of prayer and solitude, I construct a schedule to guide my time alone. I set aside time for reflective listening, journaling, and prayer, and I end the time in worship.

DAY OF SOLITUDE

You may want to plan your day according to the following guide. I recommend that you spend about an hour on each activity.

1. Begin by praising God with worship music. Feel free to sing or dance. Scripture tells us to "enter his gates with thanksgiving and his courts with praise" (Psalm 100:4).

2. Take time for reflective listening. Use one of these ideas to help you get started:

    - As you listen to worship music, ask the Holy Spirit to allow your emotions to surface.

    - Sit quietly, paying attention to what you are feeling.

    - Journal. Ask yourself, *What bothers me most about myself today? What wound am I most longing for Christ to heal in my life? With whom am I angry?*

3. Read any story from one of the Gospels and ask yourself, *Who in this passage can I most relate to and why?* Describe the feelings you perceive in that person and how those feelings correlate with your own.

4. Make a list of all the evidence that you are growing and maturing in Christ.

5. Construct a timeline of your life, charting how God has brought good out of evil.

6. Spend one hour dreaming and journaling about what you would like your life to look like in five years.

7. Take a bubble bath and worship the Lord, thanking Him that He will bring His work in you to completion. Or dance before the Lord with joy and thanksgiving—celebrate who you are becoming.

Solitude, however good, is not meant to be an end itself. God wants us to move out from our solitude into meaningful, life-giving relationships with others. Solitude enables us to find and embrace ourselves and refresh and renew ourselves in God so that we can move away from our solitude with energy to invest in others.

LEARN TO BE AT HOME WITH OTHERS IN COMMUNITY

Remember, we were designed and created for community. We are meant to be in life-giving relationships that offer encouragement, support, friendship, and love. And through these relationships, we receive those same things in return. Our relationships bring beauty and belonging to our lives. This is part of the abundant life Jesus promised (see John 10:10). One way to experience community with a friend is to spend a day together in prayer. When we mutually seek God, our hearts are knit together in new ways. Our burdens seem lighter and our joys deeper as we enter the throne room of God.

DAY OF PRAYER WITH A FRIEND

- Spend time together in worship, and ask the Holy Spirit to govern your time.

- Read a psalm out loud together.

- Spend an hour apart, journaling your individual reflections on the psalm. Then come back together and share your reflections with each other.

- Share the answers to the following questions:

  1. What is the greatest challenge you are facing at this moment?

  2. What has been your greatest struggle this past week?

  3. How has God met you?

- Spend time in prayer for each other. Pray for specific needs.

- List together some of the character traits you see in Jesus. Which character trait of His do you want to see developed in your life? Spend time in prayer together asking God to develop these character traits in each of your lives.

- Take turns sharing two hopes you have for the future, and then spend time in prayer committing these hopes to the Lord. Brainstorm what it would take to see these dreams come true.

- Separate for a half hour and write a blessing for each other.

- Reunite and pray the prayer of blessing you wrote over your friend.

Jesus modeled living in community throughout His earthly ministry. He felt at home with the Father and with Himself, and He continually invested in relationships with others. He spent time offering Himself to the crowds, building camaraderie with His disciples, and opening His soul with a few confidants. He modeled a sense of divine rhythm, spending time with people and then withdrawing for time alone with the Father. He knew He was God and felt at home with Himself. He didn't feel the need to continually prove Himself to others. Instead, He adopted the posture of a servant and a friend, able to give and receive (see Philippians 2:6-7).

We too need to experience community through close friendships. How can we follow Christ's example in this while maintaining consistent time alone with the Father and taking care of family and job expectations?

This is a question I have wrestled with often. I love people and want deep relationships with them. But I frequently feel torn among many people. I have a husband, four children, women I am mentoring, women who mentor me, several close friends, many casual friends, and several neighbors with whom I want to build relationships. I need to balance time in the presence of Christ, time for myself, time with my family, and time with others. If the scale becomes tipped too much in one direction, I end up feeling exhausted and disconnected.

Your life is probably the same. In order to maintain the sense of divine rhythm that Christ modeled, we need to know our priorities and develop an intentional plan. It helps to envision our life in terms of concentric circles of community, where each circle represents different relationships we have.

Circle A, at the center, represents our relationship with Christ. Every other relationship flows out of our communion with Him. We need enough time in His presence to fill up and flow out.

Circle B, which surrounds the center circle, represents family. If we are married, our next priority is to cultivate our relationship with our husband and then with our children. This means prioritizing time to pray for them, listen and talk to them, help them, and play with them. If we feel disconnected with a family member, we can intentionally plan some time alone with that person so that we can hear his or her heart and restore our sense of connection. Single women might prioritize time with parents, siblings, and nieces and nephews.

Circle C represents a core group of close friends. This is a handful of confidantes with whom we enjoy mutual vulnerability. Many times these are women we commit to for life. We need to schedule time to be with them, even if they live in other areas of the country.

Circle D represents those women whose companionship and camaraderie we enjoy. They are precious friends, coworkers in ministry, and women we enjoy sharing life with.

Circle E represents the community at large. This circle might include women in our neighborhood, women we meet at the health club, women whose children play sports with ours, or women who are friends of a friend.

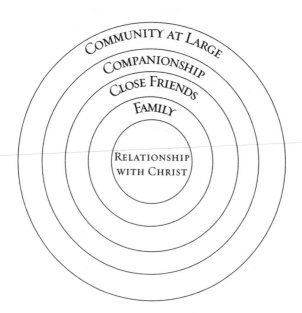

Once we have identified the people in each of these circles, we can design a plan to spend time with them. For example, Eileen, the young mom mentioned in chapter 3, longed to foster a sense of community among the women in her neighborhood. So once a month, she hosts a Girls Night Out in her home. She invites all the women in her neighborhood for a time of relaxation and fun. She serves light refreshments, leads a casual discussion, and plays a game. The women love it and come excited about the opportunity to feel connected with other women.

Jodi made some close friends in college, but they scattered all over the country. Not wanting to lose touch, these women committed to get together one weekend a year. Though they are all raising children, they meet at a resort once a year for a time of fun, fellowship, and friendship while their husbands take care of the kids.

Jill sets aside one night per week to meet with different friends she is mentoring. Mary gets together with a group of four intimate friends once a month to talk and pray about what's going on in their lives.

If we pay attention to our relationships, we can be purposeful about nurturing them rather than just leaving them to chance.

A REMINDER TO COME HOME

The next time you feel lonely, isolated, or like you don't belong, don't run or hide from those feelings. Instead, recognize and acknowledge them, and then run as fast as you can to the Father and ask Him what you need at that moment. Perhaps He will show you that you need to nestle down and relish the presence of the Holy Spirit as your constant companion. Or perhaps the time has come for you to nourish your soul by scheduling some "alone time" with Him. Or maybe you need to reach out and nurture a particular friendship. I am confident that if you long to return home, He will show you the way.

CHAPTER 8

PLEASE, SET ME FREE!

"I am . . . the truth."

JOHN 14:6

The instant I heard glass shattering and a soft thud, I knew something was very wrong. Racing downstairs, I discovered my beautiful teenage daughter unconscious on the floor. Her frail body lay in a crumpled heap, surrounded by sharp fragments of broken glass that once formed the pitcher she had been carrying.

My heart pounded as Steve and I rushed her to the emergency room. As I waited anxiously while the doctor examined her, my mind wandered back over the last couple of months. Our daughter had been limiting her calories and increasing her amount of exercise because she was convinced that she was overweight. I knew that her obsession with diet and exercise had caused her collapse. She had been caught in a deadly dieting trap.

I also knew that how I responded would either help or hinder her recovery. The stakes were high. I had been a key player in my daughter's distorted thinking about her body, and if I wanted to help her, I had to take a hard but honest look at myself. Even though I didn't starve myself, I had embraced the thought patterns of an anorexic. I used dieting to regain a sense of control whenever it felt as if my life were out of control, all the while whitewashing my behavior by telling myself that I was simply exercising self-discipline. After all, discipline is a *good thing*! My warped thinking patterns, though subtle, had caused me to ride a continual merry-go-round of counting calories, scanning fat labels, and trying numerous diet gimmicks. My daughter's collapse forced me to admit the truth: I had been modeling a dangerous and life-threatening lie — the lie that being a woman means being on a perpetual diet.

I knew I needed professional help, so I scheduled an appointment with a counselor experienced in helping women with eating disorders. During one of our conversations, my counselor challenged me to throw out our bathroom scale. My horrified response told both of us just how much my sense of security was wrapped up in my body image. I needed the God of truth to help me gain freedom from the lies I had been telling myself for so long. In one of His most powerful claims, Jesus declared, "I am . . . the truth" (John 14:6). When we bring Him the lies we have told ourselves, He gently enables us to embrace truth and find freedom.

DECEPTION CAN LOOK SO GOOD

How easy it is to deceive ourselves, even as Christian women. Deep down many of us don't want to know the truth; we prefer living in ignorance or denial. We don't want to admit that our inner world is not as orderly as we might like to project to others. We fear that admitting the truth about ourselves will mean loss of respect, loss of an image, or even loss of love. But as I know from experience, if we continue to deny the truth, we never find healing and freedom. Christ, who is truth, came to help us face the truth about ourselves and find the route to freedom.

I'm convinced that the degree to which we embrace Jesus' claim to be truth determines how victorious our Christian walk will be because every sin begins with a lie. As the Great Deceiver, Satan loves nothing more than to get us tangled up in a web of deceit. He is "the father of lies" (John 8:44), and his ways are crafty and subtle. He twists our thinking and leads us to deceive ourselves, saying such things as:

- I am in control. I can stop whenever I want.

- I will never be victorious. I've struggled with this habit for too long. I may as well give up.

- I deserve to have my emotional needs met. This extramarital relationship makes me feel happy.

- I can't change. I was born this way.

- I'm not as bad as other people; besides, everyone struggles with these thoughts.

On and on our list of excuses goes until we feel unable to extricate ourselves from our sinful behavior. Jesus came to save us from deception. He promised that those who embraced Him as the truth would find freedom: "If you continue in my word, you are truly my disciples, and you will know the truth, and the truth will make you free. . . . If the Son makes you free, you will be free indeed" (John 8:31-32,36, RSV).

TRUTH AND FREEDOM

Truth and freedom go hand in hand. If you are looking for freedom from sinful patterns of destructive behavior, you must live in obedience to Jesus' words and rely on them as truth. The Bible is *the* moral measuring stick for right and wrong, the Word of God. Anything we believe or act on that is contrary to Scripture is a lie.

Jesus said, "I am . . . *the* truth" (emphasis added). Please notice the definite article *the*. In the original Greek, the meaning of Jesus' statement is undeniable. He boldly claimed, "I am Yahweh, God with you. I am *the* truth about God, you, and life itself." He claimed to be absolute truth. As Lloyd John Ogilvie explains, "The Greek word used for truth here implies undistorted reality."[1] Don't miss the importance! As absolute truth, Jesus exposes every false idea about God, religion, and life. He is completely undistorted and as such possesses all moral authority. Because He is the Spirit of truth, He awakens our minds and explains the truth of God's Word (see John 14:26; 16:13), which is "spirit and . . . life" (John 6:63).

Your Savior longs to set you free. The chains of secrecy have held you captive for too long. He wants you to live in freedom, authenticity, and even transparency. He longs to change your thinking with His truth.

Perhaps you are thinking, *I don't tell myself lies.* That might be true about most things, but most of us are guilty of lying to ourselves at some level. We're just so used to the lie that we don't recognize it for what it is! Will you ask God's Spirit to help you recognize if you are engaging in any of these destructive patterns?

Let's take a closer look at the kinds of lies that initially seem appealing to us as women but will ultimately hurt us and those we care about and influence.

LIES ABOUT OUR BODIES

The lies we tell ourselves about our bodies are often propagated by the media and marketing experts. Advertisements tell us that if we follow certain diets, join a health club, and use the right cosmetics or have cosmetic surgery, we can achieve the perfect body of a model photographed and airbrushed in some magazine. The truth, however, is that even if we get in shape, get Botoxed, or have a tummy tuck, we will not look like a seventeen-year-old supermodel, particularly if we've given birth to several children! Nothing has ever been created that can reverse the aging process. It ain't going to happen, girlfriend! We are going to grow older . . . no matter what we do to disguise the process.

Despite this fact, more and more women are buying into the media's pitch for cosmetic surgery. While this is a private matter between you and God, I want to issue a word of caution. Surgeries are never without risk and are usually expensive. Before you decide to undergo some form of cosmetic surgery, do what Laura did. Spend some time in prayer, carefully considering your motives.

When Laura asked me if I felt it would be wrong for her to have breast enhancement surgery, I asked her to tell me more about why she wanted to have this surgery. That's when she confided in me that the boyfriend she was considering marrying had an addiction to pornography and was telling her that if she had the surgery it might help him overcome his addiction because she would be more attractive to him. I never gave Laura an answer. Instead, I told her to talk with God about it and ask for His help in evaluating her motives. After praying about what she should do, Laura decided not to have the surgery. She realized that if her boyfriend was putting pressure on her to have breast surgery — and had a problem with pornography addiction — he wasn't the kind of man she wanted to marry.

Our culture and the media tell us that our value as women lies in keeping our bodies looking young. But God's Word tells us the truth: "Do you not know that your body is a temple of the Holy Spirit, who is in you . . . ? Therefore honor God with your body" (1 Corinthians 6:19-20). Our value is not wrapped up in the size of our waists, breasts, or buttocks but rather in the fact that our bodies are God's priceless temples. When we take care of our temples, we reflect well on the owner, Jesus Christ, and bring Him honor. We do this by eating and exercising in ways that are healthy and by looking as good as is reasonably possible.

Many women find healthy eating to be one of life's biggest challenges, whether their struggle is with overeating, compulsive undereating (anorexia), or bingeing and purging (bulimia). While some may be trapped in constant dieting, others are trapped in continual overeating. This was the case in Jackie's life.

Jackie laughed as she told me that she had eaten an entire cake the night before. But I knew her laughter was an effort to hide her shame. She had always been overweight, but when her husband died, grief overwhelmed her, and she took comfort in food. In fact, she just couldn't seem to stop eating, and before long she had gained fifty pounds. When her doctor warned her that if she wanted to stay healthy, she must stick with the weight-reduction plan he had given her, she finally owned up to the truth about herself: She was a compulsive overeater — and it was killing her.

Admitting this truth liberated Jackie to make herself accountable to her doctor and to follow through on her weight-reduction plan. She began to fill her mind with what God's Word has to say about her body and how He views food. She fed her mind with verses such as, "'Everything is permissible for me' — but not everything is beneficial. . . . I will not be mastered by anything" (1 Corinthians 6:12). She prayed, "Lord, help me to know what foods are beneficial for my health. Increase my appetite for your words. I want to eat your words. They are to be my joy and delight" (see Jeremiah 15:16). As she feasted on "the fruit of the Spirit" (Galatians 5:22-23), she was reminded that the Holy Spirit desires to produce self-control in her life.

Finally, Jackie learned to go to Jesus rather than to food for comfort — and His comfort has proved to be much more fulfilling and satisfying than chocolate cake could ever be!

If you have battled an eating disorder, you know how discouraging it can be. Perhaps you are ready to give up. I understand, but I also know that victory is possible. Jackie and I are living proof that God can set you free from the lies you may tell yourself about your body. If you are fighting this battle, remember that the method God will use and the amount of time it will take to set you free are up to Him. Healing begins when we admit we have a problem and start claiming Scripture as truth over an area of weakness.

However, for complete freedom from an eating disorder, you may need the help of an experienced professional. That was the case for me, and I'm so thankful I did not let my pride get in the way or allow myself to believe another lie — the lie that it's a sin for Christians to seek professional counseling.

SUGGESTIONS FOR MOTHERS OF TEENS STRUGGLING WITH EATING DISORDERS

Food-related battles are especially serious for teenage girls. The statistics are staggering. If you have a teenage daughter, *stay alert*. Often, when patterns of eating disorders surface in teenage girls, parents are hesitant to admit there is a problem. They would prefer to keep up a false façade of being "the perfect family." This is a huge mistake. Eating disorders are addictive, and the fears lurking behind them are complex and varied.

Marian Eberly, vice president of Patient Care Services at Remuda Ranch (an eating-disorder clinic in Wickenburg, Arizona), offers these suggestions for mothers of teenage girls:[2]

Signs and Symptoms to Look For

- Weight loss of fifteen or more pounds over two to three months, accompanied by feelings of exhilaration when others might feel concerned
- Preoccupation with scales, weight, calories, or diet products
- Tendency to skip meals or appear to eat when in reality she does not
- Frequent bathroom breaks during or immediately following dinner
- Loss of menstrual period

- Intolerance of cold
- Obsessive exercise
- Depression, anxiety, irritability, and increased obsessions
- Addiction to caffeine, sometimes drinking two to three liters of diet soda per day
- Use of laxatives or diet pills

Personality Profile of a Teen Prone Toward Eating Disorders

- Perfectionist
- Driven by high standards that she sets for herself
- Very intelligent
- Very responsible
- Low self-esteem

What to Do If You Suspect Your Daughter Might Be Struggling

- Address your concerns with your daughter
- Take her to see a professional counselor
- Be prepared for an argument
- Model healthy balanced eating

If you suspect your daughter may be struggling, you may call Remuda Ranch at 1-800-445-1900.

LIES ABOUT OUR SPENDING

The minute I picked up the phone, Darla blurted out, "Well, I melted all my credit cards in the oven this afternoon. They're unusable — all melted into one big clump."

While Darla's actions may seem a bit drastic, her decision to destroy her credit cards represented a serious commitment to the truth about her addiction to shopping. Enticed by the lie of instant gratification, Darla had been using credit cards to purchase whatever she desired, even if she couldn't afford it and it meant going into debt and having to pay interest. When she heard my husband preach a sermon on stewardship, powerfully stressing the truth about God's perspective on debt, she admitted she had a problem. The Holy Spirit took the verses Steve used and pierced Darla's heart, helping her see the sin of overspending.

God's Word gives us some clear principles concerning stewardship, serving, and spending. Here are just a few:

- *Stewardship.* All that we have has been given to us by the Lord and belongs to Him (see Psalm 24:1). We are simply stewards or managers of His money, and some day He will expect an account of how we have used His resources (see Luke 19:11-26).

- *Serving.* We have been given the responsibility of serving others with the resources God has given us. Jesus had more to say about our responsibility to use our money wisely, especially by giving to the poor, than any other topic (see Luke 12:15; 16:13; 18:22). We can serve God in many ways, including with our finances. It's important to realize that if God has blessed us with much, He also expects us to use our surplus to bless others. Many mission agencies are longing for committed Christians to accept the call of God to give so that others can eat, enjoy medical care, and know Jesus Christ.

- *Spending.* God's Word clearly teaches that we are to live disciplined lives of self-control (see 1 Corinthians 9:25; Proverbs 16:32). It calls us to cultivate a life of contentment (see 1 Timothy 6:6). To do this, we might need to reign in our spending and analyze how we are managing the resources God has given us. Credit card debt puts us in bondage (see Proverbs 22:7; Romans 13:5).

Keep in mind that financial wisdom says we can go into debt in order to make a purchase that can be considered an investment, such as the purchase of a home or business. Many Christian financial experts also sanction going into debt to purchase a car. The problem comes when we go into debt to purchase items on a whim or on our wish list.

If you have fallen into the trap of overspending, Jesus longs to set you free — free from the strangling hold of debt and free to bless others. Step out of denial and into the truth.

LIES ABOUT OUR EMOTIONAL OR SEXUAL ENTANGLEMENTS

Rhonda told me, "I never thought it could happen to me!" After twenty-five years of marriage, she had engaged in an adulterous affair with a man from her church. Both committed Christians and active in ministry, they initially had no intention of letting things go so far. How did this happen?

Looking back, Rhonda says that she believed *she* could never commit adultery; after all, she was a mature believer. However, she let her guard down because Jake was so captivating. His godliness set such an example to others that she felt naturally drawn to him. He listened to her dreams, talked with her about God, and even prayed with her — and he made her laugh. Every time she would question whether what they were doing was okay, Satan would whisper, "The relationship is innocent." Soon innocent flirting yielded to passionate fondling, and passionate fondling led to secret sexual rendezvous followed by intense feelings of guilt and shame.

The result: a broken marriage, a betrayed husband, a disillusioned teenage daughter, and a truckload of guilt!

In order to free ourselves from sexual traps, we need to embrace God's truth about the wonderful gift of sexual intimacy. God reserves sexual intimacy for a husband and wife's mutual enjoyment and pleasure within the context of marriage (see Proverbs 5:15-19; Colossians 3:5,7-8). Any sexual involvement outside the confines of marriage is wrong. When we twist God's truth to rationalize our behavior, we deceive ourselves.

Jesus spoke even stronger words concerning sexual immorality: "You have heard that it was said, 'Do not commit adultery.' But I tell you that anyone who looks at a woman lustfully has already committed adultery with her in his heart" (Matthew 5:27-28). Wow! Jesus powerfully teaches that sexual sin begins in our minds, whether we are married or single. While we cannot stop temptation from entering our minds, we can refuse to dwell on the temptation. When we allow our minds to snuggle in, becoming all comfy and cozy with lust, the end result is a flaming-hot affair of the mind. How do we have these affairs of the heart and mind? We have them when we lust after emotional intimacy, spiritual intimacy, or physical intimacy with another person who is not ours to have.

Do you find yourself wishfully dreaming about such a person and then rationalizing by telling yourself that it's okay to fantasize? When we rationalize, we lie to ourselves. If you are married, fantasizing about a man other than your husband is sin. If you are single, it's wrong for you to fantasize about a married man or to entertain sexual fantasies about a single man. Paul warns, "But among you there must not be even a *hint of sexual immorality*, or of any kind of impurity, or of greed, because these are improper for God's holy people" (Ephesians 5:3, emphasis added).

When we fall into sexual sin, we pay a high price, as do those who are closest to us. Though sin is not weighted in God's eyes, it seems that the ramifications of sexual sin are more serious and far-reaching than that of other sins. If you are stepping near the edge by flirting with temptation, flee and tell! Don't keep it a secret. Dare to tell the truth to yourself, God, and a mature Christian woman.

LIES ABOUT OUR GOSSIP

Every time Tamara and Shelly met for coffee, Shelly became uncomfortable. Tamara used their coffee times to talk about her "concerns" over church leadership and, more specifically, their new pastor. He certainly didn't seem to have the same preaching abilities as the previous pastor. What had the church leadership been thinking when they called him anyway? Tamara had "heard" many members were leaving, and it didn't surprise her. After all, who wants to listen to a boring sermon? And the pastor's wife! She didn't even stand in the foyer to greet people on Sunday. Tamara said she had even heard the new pastor and his wife were having marital struggles.

"Concerns" like the ones Tamara shared with Shelly are called gossip. Gossip is listed as one of the sins that God hates. According to Proverbs 6:16-19, a gossip spreads false rumors and also engages in conversation that stirs up dissension. (I would say that Tamara's words caused dissension; wouldn't you?)

Paul instructs Timothy that one qualification for church leadership is a tight rein on the leader's tongue. He writes, "Women must likewise be dignified, not malicious gossips" (1 Timothy 3:11, NASB). The New King James translation renders the phrase "malicious gossips" as "slanderers." Slanderers "are given to finding fault with the demeanor and conduct of others and spreading their innuendos and criticisms in the church."[3]

Satan is having a field day with gossip in the American church. He delights to see church leaders wrapped up in rumor control rather than focusing on those who are dying without Christ. The Word of God calls those who gossip "fools" and instructs us to have nothing to do with them (see Proverbs 10:18; 18:6-8; 20:19). Let's step out of denial and call gossip what it is: sin. God calls us to a higher way, the way of love. If you have a "concern," God's Word lays out a clear path in Matthew 18:15-19 for how to deal with it. Go to the person in private and tell him or her your concern. If the person won't listen and you are *sure* there is sin involved, take one or two others and confront the individual again. If there is still no repentance, then take the sin to the church leaders. If you haven't gone to the person in private, don't make it public.

Amy Carmichael, one of the great early missionaries, offers these three questions as gossip sieves. Before we talk about someone else — even if it's in the form of a prayer request — let's ask ourselves:

- Is it true?
- Is it kind?
- Is it necessary?[4]

If you answer no to any of these questions, zip your lips! I wonder how much gossip would be avoided if we ran every conversation through these three sieves.

God's Word teaches us that no matter what lie has trapped us, freedom is possible.

YOUR ESCAPE ROUTE

Unlike any other book, the Bible possesses the power to change our lives (see John 17:17). God can set us free when we by faith say, "Lord, your Word is truth. I accept it as my moral standard for living." When we do this, the way we read and interpret Scripture will change because the Holy Spirit will take God's Word and make it alive in our hearts.

REVEAL

First, expose or admit the lie. When we have been deceived, we lose our perspective and can no longer view our situation or Scripture accurately. So how can we recognize those lies, particularly when Satan is so skillful at twisting our thinking? By exposing our hearts and minds to the Spirit's scrutiny. The psalmist David best illustrates this when he cries, "Search me, O God, and know my heart. . . . See if there is any offensive way in me" (Psalm 139:23-24). This goes against our human nature. When we sin, we love to hide, but the Holy Sprit calls us to exposure. The cry of our hearts each day needs to be, "Lord, search every tiny corner of my heart and show me if there is anything that offends You and Your truth."

Second Corinthians 4:2 says, "Rather, we have renounced secret and shameful ways; we do not use deception, nor do we distort the word of God." Based on this verse, there are four questions we can ask ourselves when trying to decipher any deception within us:

- Do I engage in a behavior that I hide from others?
- Do I feel ashamed about something I am doing?
- Am I twisting the truth in an effort to cover up?
- Have I distorted Scripture in order to justify my actions?

If you answered yes to any of these questions, you need to step out of denial and agree with God about that sinful behavior. I appreciate how Francis Frangipane explains this process:

> Sin wears a cloak of deception. Therefore the first stage of attaining holiness involves the exposure of our hearts to truth and the cleansing of our hearts from lies. This process of becoming holy is accomplished by the Holy Spirit, and the way the Spirit sanctifies us is with the truth. Once the Spirit breaks the power of deception in our lives, he can break the power of sin.[5]

The first step toward freedom is admitting we have a problem. From there we can move on to the second step.

REMOVE

One of the ways we take off our cloak of deception is by removing ourselves as much as possible from temptation. Most deceptive traps have some object that draws us like a magnet, pulling us with such strength that our thinking becomes twisted and rationalizing becomes easy. That object is "your temptation magnet." If you are going to live in the freedom Christ promised, you must remove that magnet. When you take the initiative to put distance between you and that object, its magnetic pull will not be as strong, and your chances of resisting will be far greater.

For example:

- If you have believed lies about your body, you may need to cancel your subscriptions to women's magazines, throw out your bathroom scale (that's what I had to do), or refrain from stocking your cupboards with particular kinds of food. It would be a good idea to memorize 1 Corinthians 6:19-20. To do so, write it on an index card and place it on your mirror. Allow the truth of those words to calm any anxious thoughts about body image. Finally, thank the Holy One that your body is a beautiful sanctuary of the One who is the truth.

- If you have fallen into patterns of fantasizing about a man other than your husband, it is imperative that you flee and tell. Remove yourself from that relationship and then ask a mature Christian woman to hold you accountable.

  If you find yourself returning to old patterns of fantasizing, run to Scripture. Memorize Philippians 2:5-8. It will help you center your thoughts on Christ and the servant attitude He wants us to adopt. This will combat the lie that says you have a "right" to have your emotional needs met in any way you can. I also recommend that you read *Every Woman's Battle* by Shannon Ethridge.

If you are single and have fallen into the trap of premarital sex, you need to find a female accountability partner and study what Scripture has to say about sexual purity. I also recommend that you read *Gift-Wrapped by God* by Linda Dillow and Lorraine Pintus.

- If you have been duped by the lie of instant gratification and have accumulated credit card debt, you may need to do what Darla did and melt your credit cards — and then resist signing up for any new ones! You may also need to cancel your catalog subscriptions and determine not to view any shopping networks. Don't go to the mall for entertainment or when you are bored.

  Since some shopping is usually necessary, you can guard against temptation by planning and prioritizing your purchases ahead of time. Write out a shopping list for groceries and other items you may need each week or month and discipline yourself to purchase only items on that list when you shop. Ask a mature friend to hold you accountable each week.

- If you struggle with gossip, make a list of the people and situations you encounter that seem to draw out this characteristic in you. Ask these individuals to work with you on this so that you can hold each other accountable. If they don't agree to this, you might want to limit your involvement with them until you feel strong enough to say, "I don't want to participate in this conversation because it is gossip." Whenever you find yourself tempted to gossip about someone, immediately turn those critical thoughts to prayer on behalf of that person.

In every deceptive trap there will always be a temptation magnet. Look for the magnet and remove it. Until you have removed that object, you will not be ready to progress to the third step.

RECLOTHE

After we have exposed the lie and distanced ourselves from the object of temptation, we are to reclothe our minds and hearts with the truth of God's Word. This is a daily process. We change our thinking by reading, meditating on, memorizing, and obeying God's Word. As we do this, the Holy Spirit renews our minds, replacing lies with truth. (Turn to page 143 for a list of Scriptures and prayers that you can use in your battle for freedom in each of these areas.)

Remember Darla, the woman who lied to herself about spending? After she melted her credit cards, she joined a small group doing a twelve-week Bible study on contentment. Each week Darla wrote in a journal the lessons she had learned from the study. As she began to reclothe her mind with truth, she meditated on Jesus' words concerning our responsibility to the poor. Darla realized she needed to be much more careful with her spending and more intentional with her giving, so she decided to give up her one cup of coffee per day at Starbucks and give that money to a mission organization that assisted orphans in Third World countries. She also asked one of the women in the study to hold her accountable. Slowly, Darla began to notice her attitudes toward spending changing and new freedom emerging.

In addition, Darla memorized Scripture verses relevant to contentment and spending and prayed them back to God, claiming victory over the temptation. For example, she memorized 1 Timothy 6:6-10:

> But godliness with contentment is great gain. For we brought nothing into the world, and we can take nothing out of it. But if we have food and clothing, we will be content with that. People who want to get rich fall into temptation and a trap and into many foolish and harmful desires that plunge men into ruin and destruction. For the love of money is a root of all kinds of evil. Some

people, eager for money, have wandered from the faith
and pierced themselves with many griefs.

Darla prayed this passage back to God, saying, "Lord Jesus, my desire
is to be godly. You know how tempted I am to spend money, but You have
said in Your Word that godliness with contentment is what You desire in
my life. Help me to flee the love of money and instead run to You and find
my contentment there."

After we have removed ourselves from the temptation magnet and
reclothed our minds with Scripture, we are ready to be restored.

RESTORE

Restoration happens in part through accountability. James 5:16 tells us to
confess our faults to one another so that we might pray for one another and
be healed. Accountability provides a safeguard against future deception. We
need spiritual mentors and accountability partners who will consistently
tell us the truth and encourage us to embrace the truth. When we place
ourselves under mature, godly leadership, we protect ourselves.

READY TO SURRENDER?

My daughter has found freedom from the eating disorder that once held
her captive. I also have experienced victory. But the temptation may
always be there. For this reason, I continue to tell my story. Whenever I
do, two things happen. First, I give God the opportunity to use it in the
life of another, and second, I remind myself that rigid control is a trap.
Even though I have experienced victory, I continue to meditate on and
memorize Scripture. On days when "fat feelings" hammer at me, I pray
God's Word and claim it over my feelings. I exchange my obsession for
truth. I also have a few close friends who hold me accountable and help
ensure that I will continue to walk in freedom.

No matter what is holding you captive, Jesus calls you to surrender and promises freedom if you will submit to His truth. Will you? If you long to be set free, I encourage you to pray this prayer: "Jesus, I bow before You and invite You to search my heart. Show me the places where I have been deceived and have become entangled. My desire is to live in the freedom You have promised. Enable me to step out of denial and into the truth of Your Word as I act in obedience and seek accountability. Help me to live in the safe shelter of Your truth."

LIST OF HELPFUL SCRIPTURES AND PRAYERS

THE TRUTH ABOUT OUR BODIES

> For a man is a slave to whatever has mastered him. (2 Peter 2:19)

> It is for freedom that Christ has set us free. Stand firm, then, and do not let yourselves be burdened again by a yoke of slavery. (Galatians 5:1)

> Therefore, I urge you, brothers, in view of God's mercy, to offer your bodies as living sacrifices, holy and pleasing to God — this is your spiritual act of worship. (Romans 12:1)

> Man does not live on bread alone but on every word that comes from the mouth of the LORD. (Deuteronomy 8:3)

> For you created my inmost being;
> you knit me together in my mother's womb.

I praise you because I am fearfully and wonderfully made;
>   your works are wonderful,
>   I know that full well.
> My frame was not hidden from you
>   when I was made in the secret place.
> When I was woven together in the depths of the earth,
>   your eyes saw my unformed body. (Psalm 139:13-16)

May God himself, the God of peace, sanctify you through and through. May your whole spirit, soul and body be kept blameless at the coming of our Lord Jesus Christ. The one who calls you is faithful and he will do it. (1 Thessalonians 5:23-24)

But you were washed, you were sanctified, you were justified in the name of the Lord Jesus Christ and by the Spirit of our God. (1 Corinthians 6:11)

Pray:

"Lord Jesus, I thank You that You formed me in my mother's womb to be a sanctuary for Your Holy Spirit. I praise You that my body has been made completely clean through the sanctifying work of Your Holy Spirit. I praise You that I don't have to live in bondage to anything because You have set me free. I offer You my body as a living sacrifice. Help me to honor You with my body."

THE TRUTH ABOUT OUR SEXUAL ENTANGLEMENTS

The body is not meant for sexual immorality, but for the Lord. . . . Flee from sexual immorality. All other sins a man commits are outside his body, but he who sins sexually sins against his own body. . . . Therefore honor God with your body. (1 Corinthians 6:13,18,20)

Dear children, do not let anyone lead you astray. (1 John 3:7)

Put to death, therefore, whatever belongs to your earthly nature: sexual immorality, impurity, lust, evil desires and greed, which is idolatry. (Colossians 3:5)

They exchanged the truth of God for a lie. . . . Because of this, God gave them over to shameful lusts. Even their women exchanged natural relations for unnatural ones. (Romans 1:25-26)

No temptation has seized you except what is common to man. And God is faithful; he will not let you be tempted beyond what you can bear. But when you are tempted, he will also provide a way out so that you can stand up under it. (1 Corinthians 10:13)

Pray:
"Holy One, thank You for the wonderful gift of sexual intimacy. Help me to keep my heart and body pure by reserving the gift of sexual intimacy for my husband alone. Guard my heart and keep me from exchanging the truth of God's laws for a lie. When I find myself tempted by sexual entanglements, remind me that there is no temptation greater than what I can handle with Your Spirit's power. Thank You for Your promise to always provide a way out."

The Truth About Our Spending

"No one can serve two masters. Either he will hate the one and love the other, or he will be devoted to the one and despise the other. You cannot serve both God and Money." (Matthew 6:24)

For the love of money is a root of all kinds of evil. Some people, eager for money, have wandered from the faith and pierced themselves with many griefs. (1 Timothy 6:10)

Keep your lives free from the love of money and be content with what you have. (Hebrews 13:5)

"Watch out! Be on your guard against all kinds of greed; a man's life does not consist in the abundance of his possessions." (Luke 12:15)

The borrower is servant to the lender. (Proverbs 22:7)

Pray:
"Lord Jesus, Your Word tells me that I am to keep my life free from the love of money. Help me to understand the truth that greed is a form of idolatry and debt is a form of bondage. Help me to serve You with the resources You have given me."

The Truth About Our Gossip

"Do not spread false reports." (Exodus 23:1)

Whoever spreads slander is a fool. (Proverbs 10:18)

When words are many, sin is not absent. (Proverbs
10:19)

The lips of the righteous nourish many,
    but fools die for lack of judgment. (Proverbs 10:21)

But to the wicked, God says: . . .
"You use your mouth for evil
    and harness your tongue to deceit.
You speak continually against your brother
    and slander your own mother's son."
    (Psalm 50:16,19-20)

A fool's mouth is his undoing,
    and his lips are a snare to his soul.
The words of a gossip are like choice morsels;
    they go down to a man's inmost parts.
    (Proverbs 18:7-8)

"But the things that come out of the mouth come from
the heart, and these make a man [or woman] 'unclean.'
For out of the heart come evil thoughts, murder,
adultery, sexual immorality, theft, false testimony,
slander." (Matthew 15:18-19)

Pray:
    *"Holy One, You have called the one who gossips a
fool. I desire that my tongue honor Your name by bringing
healing and refreshment to others. Teach me to strain my
words through Amy Carmichael's three sieves and to walk
away when others try to gossip to me. My desire is not to
please man but You alone."*

CHAPTER 9

BUT
I CAN'T!

"I am the vine."

JOHN 15:5

I paced back and forth in my hotel room, sure that the conference directors had made a mistake. The other speakers were famous, distinguished authors, and I, on the other hand, well . . . I was just *me*.

Initially, I felt excited about being asked to speak at such a well-known conference for Christian leaders. The awesome opportunity immediately prompted me to rejoice, thanking God for the chance to be His vessel. In the previous months, I had asked God to show me the message He would have me give, and I felt good about the upcoming conference — until I found out who the other speakers were. The moment I began comparing myself to them, my confidence and courage crumbled as feelings of inadequacy and self-doubt rushed in.

Praying my husband would pick up his cell phone, I called Steve. "The other speakers are good — *really* good. They've all written books — *many* books. I can't speak. I'm afraid I won't be as good as the other speakers."

"Becky, listen to me." Steve's voice held enough confidence for us both. "God gave you this message. Don't compare yourself to the others. This is your time to shine. I'll be praying. Knock 'em dead, Babe."

At that moment, I realized I had lost my connection. Not my cell phone connection, but a much more vital one. The static of my own insecurities had interrupted my clear connection with Jesus as the vine. I had lost the small whisper of the Spirit's voice.

I hung up the phone, knelt down, and confessed that in my anxiousness, I had become self-focused instead of God-focused. I prayed, "Holy One, I confess to You that I have measured my abilities against the gifts of others. I feel so inadequate, but I know this is Your message, not mine. You have said that You alone are the vine. I'm only the branch You are using — and a very weak one at that. I want to bring glory to Your name tonight. I don't want my nervousness to block the flow of Your Spirit's power. Speak through me, Holy Spirit. I give You my mouth."

I had to let go, abandoning myself to be used by the One who said, "Not by might nor by power, but by my Spirit" (Zechariah 4:6).

LET ME COUNT THE WAYS . . .

Feelings of inadequacy and self-doubt can attack our minds at a moment's notice. "I can't" reverberates through our thoughts like an ominous echo. We say, "I can't" in many different ways:

- It's our cry of despair when our marriage is faltering and love seems impossible.

- It's our groan of despondency when all our parenting techniques have failed with a rebellious teen.

- It's our sigh of dread at the thought of going through another year as a single woman.

- It's our moan of defeat when considering the daunting task of forgiveness.

- It's our grunt of discouragement when we feel overwhelmed by the amount or type of work that needs to be done.

- It's our whimper of disbelief after hearing a diagnosis that means raising a special-needs child.

If left unchecked, our protests of "But, Lord, I can't!" drown out the quiet, sweet voice of the Holy Spirit who whispers, "I can." How can we replace feelings of inadequacy and self-doubt with holy confidence? The answer lies in abiding, in staying closely connected to the life-giving power of the Holy Spirit. This is the message of John 15.

IT'S ALL ABOUT ABIDING

Several summers ago, my times alone with the Lord felt strained. Though I consistently kept them with rigid discipline, they felt stale and dry. My appointments with God felt like just another daily ritual to be checked off at the beginning of each day.

Desperate for something fresh and alive, I set aside my normal Bible reading schedule for the summer and turned my attention to John 15. I typed and printed out the entire passage in double-space format so I could circle key words and phrases. As I interacted with the passage, recording my questions and observations, I realized my relationship with Christ had taken a beating. I had been trying so hard for so long to do everything I could to grow as a Christian and be more like Christ. I kept prayer lists in an effort to be sure I covered everyone. I targeted different character traits, trying to change my attitudes so that I felt loving, peaceful, and joyful. I served God faithfully wherever I could. But after a while, instead of enjoying my relationship with Christ, I felt overwhelmed, exhausted, and discouraged.

As I studied John 15, I made a startling discovery — the branch never seemed to be stressed out! The branch simply *rested*, living and depending on the vine to do all the work.

I wanted that rest, so I asked the Holy Spirit to make the words of John 15 come alive in my heart and to show me exactly how to reignite the intimacy I had once enjoyed with Him. His answer sounded so simple that it surprised me: "Let Me do the work. You just stay close."

Jesus' words reveal the secret of approaching with confidence a task or challenge for which we seem unprepared and inadequate. Jesus proclaimed, "I am the vine; you are the branches. If [you *remain*] in me and I in [you], [you] will bear much fruit; *apart from me you can do nothing*" (John 15:5, emphasis added). When we learn how to abide in Jesus as the vine, He does His work through us. Jesus takes our inadequacy and self-doubt and replaces it with holy confidence. We know that He will enable us to do whatever He asks of us. This is the incredible promise of John 15.

Let's take a closer look at this passage to learn what it means to abide.

IMAGES FROM A VINEYARD

Jesus was preparing the disciples for His imminent departure. He knew that when He ascended into heaven to take His place with the Father, He would be leaving the disciples with an impossible task: "Go and make disciples of all nations" (Matthew 28:19). These uneducated and unpolished fishermen would have the extraordinary job of founding the early church.

What was Jesus thinking? Certainly He could have come up with a stronger team to launch the early church! A more inadequate group would be hard to imagine. James and John argued over who would be the greatest in the kingdom. Thomas wrestled with constant doubt. Peter struggled with continually putting his foot in his mouth. How could this ragtag group be transformed into the preachers, teachers, healers, and writers they needed to be in order to change the world with the message of Jesus and His forgiveness?

Jesus knew panic would envelop them if He did not give them a clear picture of their position in Him. So He used images from a vineyard to reassure their frightened hearts, as well as to teach them — and us — that He could help them accomplish what He had asked them to do. Jesus told them,

> "I am the true vine, and my Father is the gardener. He cuts off every branch in me that bears no fruit, while every branch that does bear fruit he prunes so that it will be even more fruitful. You are already clean because of the word I have spoken to you. Remain in me, and I will remain in you. No branch can bear fruit by itself; it must remain in the vine. Neither can you bear fruit unless you remain in me. I am the vine; you are the branches. If [you remain] in me and I in [you], [you] will bear much fruit; apart from me you can do nothing." (John 15:1-5)

Let's take a moment to clarify who's who and what's what in this vineyard.

- Jesus is the vine. "I am the true vine" (verse 1). The vine, or trunk of the plant, grows up out of the ground, supporting and sustaining all the gnarly branches that grow out in every direction. Israel, referred to in the Old Testament as the "vineyard of the LORD Almighty," failed to produce righteous fruit (Isaiah 5:1-7). Jesus, however, came as the perfect vine, able to sustain and produce righteous fruit in everyone who remains in Him.

- God is the gardener. "My Father is the gardener" (verse 1). As the gardener, God plants, positions, and prunes the vine. He carefully coaxes as much fruit from the vine as possible. The vine lives totally dependent on the gardener.

- You are the branch. "I am the vine; you are the branches" (verse 5).
  A branch is simply a bit of wood brought forth by the vine to bear
  the fruit of the vine. The branch lives in complete dependence on
  the vine, drawing from it its very life and nourishment.

- The fruit is good works or Christlike attitudes. "If [you remain]
  in me and I in [you], [you] will bear much fruit" (verse 5). Paul
  instructs, "Let our people also learn to maintain good works, to
  meet urgent needs, that they may not be unfruitful" (Titus 3:14,
  NKJV). Actions such as sharing our faith or tangibly meeting
  someone's physical needs could be classified as "external fruit."
  Paul also says the fruit of the Spirit are the attitudes of "love, joy,
  peace, patience, kindness, goodness, faithfulness, gentleness and
  self-control" (Galatians 5:22-23). Changed attitudes that bring
  us closer to the likeness of Christ could be classified as "internal
  fruit." For instance, we may be anxious and worried whenever we
  have to do something out of our comfort zone. But over time, if we
  consistently abide in Christ and ask the Holy Spirit to change us,
  He will replace our anxiety with peace.

Jesus says we will produce lasting fruit when we are connected to the
Vine. What happens to a branch if it gets cut off from the vine? It dies.
The only way a branch can thrive and bear fruit is by *abiding* in the vine.
Jesus told this story in order to drive home a similar point to His disciples:
Stay connected to God, and He will help you accomplish what He's asked
you to do.

So what does it look like for the twenty-first-century woman to
abide? To abide, we must:

- Confess our attempts to be the vine
- Surrender to His pruning

- Cultivate a continual sense of Christ's nearness
- Allow Him to flow through us to others

My prayer is that you will choose to do these things and as a result will discover the joy of a life of fruitful abundance.

CONFESS OUR ATTEMPTS TO BE THE VINE

When we forget our role as the branch and try to usurp the role of the Vine:

- We become frustrated, trying to earn holiness through our own self-efforts rather than depending on God's power and grace to change us.

- We become manipulative, trying to change those around us rather than allowing the Holy Spirit to change them.

- We become tense, trying to depend on our own gifts and abilities rather than looking to God to help us.

- We become frazzled, trying to control our lives rather than giving control over to Him.

Do any of these attitudes sound familiar? If so, then you are living life in what I call The Uptight Zone — and have usurped the role of the Vine in your life. When our lives lack the internal fruit of the Spirit — love, joy, peace, and patience — it's a sure indicator that we are not abiding in Christ.

Whenever we usurp the role of the Vine, it results in dissatisfaction and failure. We were created to be the branch. A branch simply cannot produce fruit on its own. It is completely dependent on the vine. This is why Jesus emphasized to His followers, "Apart from me you can do nothing" (15:5).

God does not expect us to be the vine. Instead, He calls us to be a branch grafted into the true vine. Just as a cutting is first severed from its old vine, we have been severed from our old life of self-effort and self-focus and have been grafted into the heart of Christ. As we abide in Him, He changes us from the inside out so that we are able to cry with Paul, "I no longer live, but Christ lives in me" (Galatians 2:20).

When this happens, our attention is drawn away from our inadequacies and refocused on His abilities. We are no longer held captive by our weaknesses but are captivated by Him. Our weaknesses compel us to "bow down and be still"[1] before Him, and we draw strength from Him and cooperate with His attempts to change us.

This is what Margaret did:

When I recognized that I often tried to be the Holy Spirit in other people's lives, pointing out areas where *they* should change, I felt devastated. For years I considered it a good thing to "encourage" others to change. I told myself I was helping them. But then God showed me that I was not only being judgmental toward others, but I was also trying to take His place in their lives. I knew I couldn't change myself, so I cried out, "Lord, change me!" I promised Him I would no longer usurp His role and would instead be more careful with my tongue. I asked Him to help me lift others up with my words and leave the role of conviction to Him.

To help me remember my commitment, I bought a small, glass hot-air balloon and put it on a shelf in my house where I would see it often. Every time my eye caught sight of the hot-air balloon, I reminded myself that Christ was present and that He wanted my words to lift others up.

I too have struggled with usurping the role of the Vine. Recently, I told a friend about my desire for someone close to me to come to Christ. My friend listened and then wisely reminded me, "Becky, it's not your job to change anyone. It's only your job to love people and share Jesus with them." Oh, how I needed that reminder. Our part is to share Christ's love with others. His part is to change them.

Jesus can be trusted to be the Vine. He doesn't need our help. What incredible assurance for those of us who feel inadequate! Author Roy Heisson reminds us, "He is never at a loss, never discouraged, never defeated, and He is our vine! Our weakness and emptiness are no hindrance to Him; indeed, they give Him the more room in which to prove Himself."[2]

If you've been trying to be God, chances are you've been doing it for a while and it has become a pattern in your life. Will you confess your efforts and ask God to change you? Yield one area at a time and depend on Him.

SURRENDER TO HIS PRUNING

Every gardener knows that pruning makes a plant more fruitful, and the same principle is true in our lives as Christians. Our Gardener lovingly cultivates each branch so that it will bear as much fruit as possible. How does He do this? He prunes. He prunes both the branches that are barren and the branches that do bear fruit.

The branch that bears no fruit has either lost its connection to the vine or is trailing on the ground, becoming bogged down and dirty. This same principle holds true in our lives. The child of God who bears no evidence of Christlikeness has likely become bogged down and dirty with sin. What does the Gardener do with a branch that bears no fruit? Jesus says, "He cuts off every branch in me that bears no fruit" (John 15:2).

Reading these words, you might be feeling a bit nervous and thinking, *Uh-oh, I'm in trouble! There hasn't been much fruit in my life lately. Does this mean Christ is going to cut off His relationship with me?* No. Many experts in Greek feel a more accurate translation of "cut off" would be "take up" or "lift up."[3]

When vineyard growers observe a branch trailing on the ground, covered with mud and mildew and ultimately sick and useless, they don't cut off the branch. Instead, they gently lift the branch up and wash it off. In the same way, when we fall into sin and stop bearing fruit, our loving Gardener lifts us up and cleans us off so that we can be free to once again bear fruit. He does this by disciplining us in order to lift us away from destructive and sinful pursuits.

His discipline may come in the form of hardship or painful circumstances. Remember Jonah, the Old Testament prophet who didn't like his God-given assignment to go to Nineveh? He took off on a ship in the opposite direction but ended up in the belly of a great fish where God could finally speak to him and have his undivided attention. After spending three days in the belly of that fish, Jonah was ready and willing to do as God had asked (see Jonah 3:1-3).

Though the Lord's discipline doesn't feel good, it is assurance of His love for us. The writer of Hebrews encourages us to not lose heart when the Lord rebukes "because the Lord disciplines those he loves" (Hebrews 12:6). His correction is intended to nudge us toward the fruitful life He intended for us.

Even when a branch bears fruit, the gardener will prune it so it can bear even more fruit. Jesus told His disciples, "Every branch that does bear fruit he prunes" (verse 2). If the branch is bearing fruit already, why prune it? Because pruning cuts it back to the place of connection with the vine and allows the connection to become enlarged. This enlargement enables more life-giving sap to pour through the branch, resulting in more fruit. For the vine to produce "much fruit," the inner life of the branch must be expanded.

The same principle applies to our lives. The Father often prunes us, precisely and perfectly, bringing us to the end of ourselves. Pruning invites us to surrender to Him and often cuts to the core of our personal identity. Though painful, this reducing of self enlarges our dependency on the life-giving power of the Holy Spirit. The less we block the connection, the more the Holy Spirit's power can flow, which results in more fruit.

How we respond to the Father's pruning ultimately influences how much fruit we will produce. Surrender is never easy, but ultimately it leads to worship as we bow our wills to His and ask only that our souls be enlarged so that we may know Him more fully.

I've recently gone through a season of intense pruning. My soul has cried, "Ouch, Lord!" At times I have looked around at other branches and argued with the Gardener, protesting, "Lord, why aren't you pruning them? Why me? I've had enough!" But He has shown me that I need more of Him and less of me. The loving Gardener has performed a deep surgery on my soul; He has cut away ministry opportunities that gave me a sense of self-worth and identity so I would find my identity in being His beloved child who does not need to perform. He has cut away relationships that provided a sense of belonging so I would find my security in Him alone. He has cut away the approval of some people that I might learn to live for an audience of One. Yet in the stripping away, He has given me Himself. My cries have changed from "No more, Lord!" to "You alone, Lord."

Has the Holy One been snipping away in your life? Can you bow before the Gardener and prayerfully set your heart on Him? You will find that as He cuts away all that competes with Him, He gives Himself.

CULTIVATE A CONTINUAL SENSE OF CHRIST'S NEARNESS

Those who enjoy deep intimacy with God cultivate a continual awareness of His presence. Their lives revolve around one priority — knowing Christ more fully. Cynthia Heald wrote,

> Deep in my heart is the constant prayer that I would be a woman who consistently walks with God. I know that apart from Christ, I can do nothing — at least nothing that is selfless, truly satisfying, and eternal. Essential to

walking with God is maintaining unbroken communion with Him.[4]

How do we maintain unbroken communion with God? We begin by intentionally setting aside time for Him.

Set Aside Time to Be with Him

I begin every morning by reading the Bible, journaling, and spending time in worship. Through these spiritual disciplines, I have learned to know the heart of Jesus more fully. I find that if I set my heart to follow Him first thing in the morning, it is easier to live in His presence all day. In the last few years I have renewed my commitment to keeping my times with Him fresh and alive.

Here are some ideas for waking up sluggish quiet times:

- Read God's Word, expecting Him to speak. Some days I leave my Bible open on an end table to remind me throughout the day of what God spoke to me that morning.

- Mark and date significant verses in your Bible. Throughout my Bible I have dates written next to verses that God has used to encourage my heart or verses I have prayed specifically over my children.

- Talk to God. Brennan Manning writes, "The only way to fail in prayer is not to show up."[5] At times I have felt at a loss not knowing how to pray for someone. I have learned to ask the Holy Spirit to guide my prayers and show me how to pray. Rather than planning my prayers, I now yield every thought to the Holy Spirit. I focus my prayers wherever my mind drifts during prayer, trusting that the Holy Spirit is guiding my thoughts. For example, I used to feel guilty for not praying for the church around the world. When I brought this desire before the Holy Spirit, He began to lay certain nations on my heart, and when He did, I would pray. Allowing Him to lead has taken all the pressure off my prayer life. He leads; I follow.

- Record the answers to your prayers. This builds faith. At the end of the year, read through all the answers to prayer and celebrate them.

- Listen for His small voice. God not only speaks through His Word, but often He speaks through His still, small voice. Learn to be still and quiet. Train yourself to listen. Start by praying, "Speak to me, Lord. I'm waiting and listening."

- Learn to linger. If you find yourself rushed, set aside time once a week, once a month, or even once a season to "luxuriate in His presence."[6] You might take a long walk or a personal retreat or lie in bed a bit longer one morning, talking to God while you are there. Teach yourself to savor each moment with the Lord.

A few years ago, my husband met with Leighton Ford, noted author and president of Leighton Ford Ministries, to ask him some questions about his spiritual walk. When Steve asked for advice about rekindling his spiritual vitality, Leighton wisely answered, "Ruthlessly eliminate hurry!" A sense of rush and hurry kills intimacy.

It takes time to cultivate a deep sense of enjoyment in God's presence, so don't give up. Tell Him of your desire to enjoy Him and then wait with expectancy until He answers.

Cultivate Your Awareness of His Presence All Day

Brother Lawrence, a seventeenth-century monk who worked in a monastery kitchen, described his practice of abiding in God by saying, "I do nothing else but abide in His Holy presence, and I do this by simple attentiveness and an habitual, loving turning of my eyes on Him. This I call . . . a wordless and secret conversation between soul and God which no longer ends."[7]

I have tried to develop this practice in my own life. All day long I have quiet conversations with the Lord. I try to acknowledge His presence in every moment. When one of my kids is hurt or angry, I beg for wisdom about what to say. When I'm writing or preparing to speak, I ask Him to flow through me. When I'm ironing my husband's shirts, I ask Him to encourage and strengthen my husband's heart. When I'm cooking dinner, I pray for neighbors or friends. Throughout the day, I express my love to Him.

Try these tips to remind yourself of God's presence throughout the day:

- Put a sticky dot in the center of your watch. When you see the sticker as you check the time throughout the day, let it remind you that God is near.

- Set apart your driving time for time alone with God. While I am driving to and from appointments or activities, I dedicate my alone time in the car for prayer and worship. Worship music in my CD player prompts my praise. I have also designated particular stoplights around town to remind me to pray for specific people.

- Pray before every appointment, asking God for wisdom.

- Put a visual reminder on your desk. Clare, a resource teacher, keeps a small New Testament on her desk to remind her of Christ's presence. She prays over each child she interacts with throughout her day.

As we grow in cultivating a continual awareness of the Holy Spirit's presence, our attitudes will change. Tension and worry will be replaced with calm. Fear and doubt will be replaced with courage. Impossible situations won't feel as overwhelming, and deadlines won't seem as dreadful. We will learn to lift our eyes from the pressure to the perfect One. Gradually we will find that if we abide in Him, He will flow through us, accomplishing all that He desires.

ALLOW HIM TO FLOW THROUGH US TO OTHERS

You might be thinking, *That sounds like a life purpose for someone who's graduated from seminary. I can't do that!* Yes, you can. You just need to become available to be an extension of Jesus in someone else's life. After all, that's the purpose of a branch — to be a living extension of the vine. You may feel inadequate to change the world, but there are many ways you can partner with God to become a living extension of Jesus to just one person at a time.

Consider a few examples of what other Christian women have done.

After the San Diego fires destroyed thousands of homes, leaving many without a place to live, Cindi wanted to do something to help those who had lost everything. The enormity of their needs left her feeling inadequate, but Cindi determined to do something. So she focused her efforts in just one neighborhood where the fires had done severe damage. She recruited and organized numerous volunteers to help sift through ashes in order to help the victims of the fire find any valuables that might be salvageable. She helped serve meals to those who were left homeless and were living in tents. Because of her compassionate actions, Cindi became a living extension of Jesus to those who were heartbroken over their incalculable losses.

Stacey allowed Christ to flow through her by volunteering in a mentoring program. She lovingly became a "big sister" to a lonely fourteen-year-old girl. Stacey bought this teenager books and clothes and took her shopping and to the movies. She has made a huge difference in one teen's life by her love and example.

Margie told me that she had felt inadequate to share Christ with her neighbor, Scott. In truth, she didn't even like him. His "alternate lifestyle" repulsed her. Then one day the Holy Spirit convicted her of her judgmental attitude, and Margie realized *she* needed to change — just as much as Scott did. She confessed her negative and unloving feelings and began praying for the opportunity to demonstrate Christ's love to Scott. God answered her prayer in an unusual way. Months later, Scott was diagnosed with AIDS. Shortly after that, his partner left him, which meant Scott was now sick and all alone. As she prayed about what she could do, Margie felt the Holy Spirit nudging her to bring Scott meals and shop for him. She set up round-the-clock medical care for him, interviewing and hiring each of the nurses. On many days Margie sat by his bed, reading Scripture to him. She told me, "I worried that somehow I might contract AIDS and give it to my husband or ten-year-old daughter. But I knew I had to trust God. Then during one of my visits, I told Scott about Christ's love — and Scott received Jesus into his life." Christ's love flowed through Margie into Scott's life because she said yes to God.

How can you allow Jesus to flow through you? Ask Him to give you a heart for those around you. You may be inadequate to change the whole world, but you can change one life at a time. Become acquainted with those in your neighborhood and community. Learn the names of those who work in your grocery store, favorite coffee shop, and gas station. Join the local gym and get to know others who work out there. Ask them by name how they are.

One of the most effective ways to partner with Christ is through the story of what He has done in your life. Write out your story so that you can communicate it clearly. Memorize two or three verses to go with it and then ask God to provide opportunities to share what He has done in your life. Remember, you are only the branch. It's not your job to change people; your job is to remain in the Vine and allow His Spirit to flow through you to others.

THE PROMISE

Those who abide in the vine become intimate friends with Christ. When they feel inadequate, they cling to Him in tighter dependency. They trust Him to produce the results through them. They look to Him to change their attitudes, and they ask Him how they can make themselves more available to others. They realize it's all about abiding!

My friend Pam recently wrote me about how utterly helpless she felt when God allowed a "difficult assignment" to come her way. Her words are a poignant reminder that God's deepest desire is not that we be adequate but that we be dependent on Him.

> I no longer believe that God doesn't give you more than you can handle. Sam, our youngest child, was a most beautiful baby boy, so when he was diagnosed with autism at age two we could hardly believe it. I knew little to nothing about autism and felt completely inadequate. All I knew to do was to begin researching and praying. I spent hours researching programs and methods. I prayed over Sam every night, and throughout the day I asked God for wisdom.

God began to answer my prayers through articles, friends, doctors, and specialists that He brought into our lives. No one person was able to outline a program, so we had to take Sam's education into our own hands. It was up to me to make calls, research programs, find special language tutors, and go to bat for Sam to prove his eligibility for state-funded programs and early-start programs.

People ask me all the time how I do it, and I say that I can't do it alone. I have to continually draw strength from a greater source than myself.

As you confess your tendency to usurp God's role in your life, surrender to His pruning, cultivate a constant sense of His closeness, and make yourself available to partner with Him, your intimate friendship with Him will grow and the Father will delight in listening to and answering your prayers.

Lord Jesus, I worship You as my Vine. I praise You that my only responsibility as the branch is to abide in You. Thank You for offering me intimate friendship. Show me what it looks like to stay close to You moment by moment. Flow through me, allowing me to be an extension of You to my husband, my children, my coworkers, and my neighbors. I am available to partner with You today.

CHAPTER 10

HOW MUCH LONGER, LORD?

"I am the Alpha and the Omega."
REVELATION 22:13

*W*e are an impatient people. If there are more than twelve people in line at Starbucks, we leave; if we get stuck behind a slow car, we flash our lights; if we are put on hold on the telephone, we hang up; if the express checkout at the grocery store is closed, we complain; if our flight is delayed, we hyperventilate. We can't stand to wait! We value microwaves, instant oatmeal, fast food, shortcuts, and instant messaging.

This was brought home to me a few months ago. I arrived at the Department of Motor Vehicles at 6:30 a.m. to ensure that I would be at the front of the line. Only two people were ahead of me. The first man had a camping chair in hand for the long wait. Very clever!

Over the next hour and a half the line grew until it wrapped around the building. When the doors to the DMV did not open at 8:00, one disgruntled man checked the schedule posted on the door. A groan arose from the crowd as he explained that because it was Wednesday and the week before Easter, the DMV would operate on "holiday schedule" and not open till 9:00. We weren't happy about it, but what could we do?

A few moments before 9:00, a shout arose from inside the building, and we watched in disbelief as one employee wearing bunny ears led the charge for an Easter egg hunt for all the DMV employees. The doors did not open until every egg had been found. Words cannot describe how angry people were that they had to stand in line for hours so the Department of Motor Vehicles could have an Easter egg hunt.

Waiting in line for hours is frustrating, especially when an Easter egg hunt takes priority over hundreds of people's busy schedules, but that kind of waiting is minor compared with much of our waiting. I think of friends and family members who are waiting right now. I have an aunt who waited for years to receive a kidney transplant and who now sits waiting for hours each week hooked up to a dialysis machine. I have a daughter praying that she will get a job, a friend praying and waiting for a marriage partner, and another who's praying for her child to come back to the Lord. During times like these, waiting tests our faith. We just want to shout, "God, will you *please* hurry up and do something?" It has been my experience that God is never in a rush, even when the situation seems to warrant it. At times, He even seems downright slow! If you look closer at Scripture, you will find this is consistent with His nature.

Jesus never turned to the disciples and said, "Will you guys please hurry up and get your sandals on? We're going to be late!" He arrived at Jairus's house after the man's daughter had already died (see Luke 8:40-56). As we saw in chapter 6, He deliberately stayed where He was two more days before responding to Mary and Martha's request to come and heal Lazarus (see John 11:6). He spent time with the Father when the disciples wanted to rush Him to meet the needs of the crowd (see Mark 1:35-37). He even kept His mother and brothers waiting while He finished preaching (see Matthew 12:47). Nowhere in the Gospels does Jesus appear hurried or distracted because of the urgency of some request.

This amazes me. Everyone I know — even the most patient people — sometimes get in a rush about *something*. I think this is an important observation because it helps us understand that God acts according to *His* timeframe, not ours. Sometimes that means He will answer our prayers quickly; other times it means we may need to wait. Think for a few moments. What have you been waiting for?

- Salvation of a loved one
- Justice for someone who has hurt you
- Direction for your future
- Healing
- Employment
- Repentance on the part of your teenager or spouse
- A loving husband
- A child of your own through pregnancy or adoption

Does it seem as if God is taking forever to answer? Be assured, He is not trying to make your life miserable. He simply holds a different perspective on forever.

GOD'S PERSPECTIVE ON FOREVER

Jesus said, "I am the Alpha and the Omega" (Revelation 22:13). Alpha and Omega are the names of the first and last letters of the Greek alphabet. With this claim Jesus was saying that before the creation of the world, before any great historical event, He existed. He is the first, but He is also the last. He is infinitely eternal, the never-ending One. The writer of Hebrews wrote, "Jesus Christ is the same yesterday and today and forever" (13:8). Moses wrote, "From everlasting to everlasting you are God" (Psalm 90:2). Isaiah called Jesus the Everlasting Father (see Isaiah 9:6). Before time began, Jesus was; and after time ends, He will continue to be. He is eternally existent—before our past and beyond our tomorrow. Not bound by time, He doesn't need a Day-Timer, a watch, or a Palm Pilot. Jesus, the Alpha and Omega, dwells forever outside time.

What are the implications of this claim for you and me, especially as we wait for God to answer our prayers? There are many, but I'd like to focus on just a few that have encouraged me when I've been weary from waiting.

THE PURPOSE OF DELAY

Although it is not always possible to know or understand God's purposes, we can trace certain patterns throughout Scripture that help us understand why He allows us to wait. The first has to do with refining us as His instruments (see Psalm 66:10-12); the second has to do with preparing the environment for His glorious works (see Psalm 105:16-22).

1. *Delay sharpens us, His instruments.* Dr. Edman, former president of Wheaton College, observed, "Delay never thwarts God's purpose; rather it polishes His instrument."[1] How does delay sharpen a person for the task God assigns? Delay becomes God's tool for deepening our humility, strengthening our faith, clarifying our vision, honing our skills, and refining our character.

David is a good example of someone whose character was refined by waiting. Probably only a teenager when anointed to be the next king of Israel, he spent the next "seven to ten years"[2] running from Saul and waiting for God to crown him king. He must have wondered if he would ever rule Israel. He passionately wrote, "How long, O LORD? Will you forget me forever?" (Psalm 13:1) and "My soul is in anguish. How long, O LORD, how long?" (Psalm 6:3)

Waiting "forced" David into deeper dependency on God. Author Bob Sorge writes this about David's life: "The years of delay, from the time of promise to the time when he actually became king, were used as a refining fire by God to purify David and prepare him for the throne."[3] We see evidence of David's growth and maturity when he had an opportunity to kill Saul, who had been hunting David down in order to kill him, but didn't because he knew that Saul was still God's anointed king. David restrained himself, sparing Saul and choosing to trust God's timing (see 1 Samuel 24:1-12). As a result of having to wait nearly a decade between being anointed king and actually being crowned king, David learned discipline and restraint — character qualities that are important in the leader of a country.

Waiting also weans us off counterfeit ego builders, such as how well we perform or how fast we produce. When self is stripped away, God can use us as He desires. When delay forces us to recognize that we are not in control, we step back and let God do whatever He wants whenever He wants to. We see this illustrated in Hannah's life.

Hannah wanted a baby more than anything and yet couldn't conceive. Year after year she prayed and wept, begging God for a son. The longer Hannah prayed, the more desperately she pressed into God for the thing she desired. Bowing before the Holy One, Hannah poured out her longings and then agreed that if God answered her request, she would give the child back to Him. God granted Hannah the desire of her heart, and as she had promised, Hannah brought Samuel to the temple, where she told the priest, "I prayed for this child, and the LORD has granted me what I asked of him. So now I give him to the LORD" (1 Samuel 1:27-28). Waiting made Hannah willing to relinquish her child, and that child grew up to be one of Israel's greatest prophets.

2. *Delay allows time for God to set the stage.* Sometimes we have to wait while God, the Producer in our life stories, arranges events and situations so that His plan for our lives can unfold. We can see how this works when we look at Joseph's life.

When he was just a boy, God gave Joseph a vision that he would someday become a great leader. Because Joseph was the eleventh child out of twelve, this idea not only sounded preposterous to his family, but it also must have sounded arrogant. Because Joseph was his father's favorite child, his older brothers harassed him and ordered him around.

When they betrayed him and sold him into slavery, Joseph landed in Egypt, where things only got worse. Eventually thrown into prison for something he didn't do, Joseph must have wondered if he had correctly interpreted the dream God had given him. After all, it was unlikely that he would ever be released from prison.

But God was up to something. He was arranging events so that Joseph could indeed become a great leader. A butcher and a baker, fellow prisoners of Joseph, both had dreams that Joseph correctly interpreted. (He said the baker would be released from prison and return to the palace to serve the Pharaoh, but the butcher would be executed.) Later, Pharaoh had a dream that no one could interpret, but the baker remembered Joseph and recommended him to Pharaoh.

Because Joseph interpreted Pharaoh's dream, the ruler was so impressed that he not only freed Joseph from prison but also gave him a position of leadership in the country that was second only to Pharaoh. When a severe famine hit the land, Joseph had the influence and power to save his father and family, who later became the nation of Israel. God used the delay in Joseph's life to set the stage for His plans for Joseph as well as for the nation of Israel.

Are you tired of waiting? Is it possible that God is setting the stage right now so that at just the right moment, He can unfold the next scene in your life? Perhaps it will be your biggest performance.

Hudson Taylor, whom I mentioned in chapter 7, became ill after six years of intense service in China. Laid up for five years in London, Hudson must have wondered if God had placed him on the shelf. But God was sharpening his servant and setting the stage for Hudson Taylor's greatest life work. During that period, Hudson birthed the vision of China Inland Mission, an organization responsible for leading thousands to Christ in China. About those long dark years of waiting on God, Taylor wrote, "Without those hidden years, with all their growth and testing, how could the vision and enthusiasm of youth have been matured for the leadership that was to be?"[4]

Don't underestimate the Producer's timing and wisdom. As He sharpens you, His instrument, He is setting the stage for the next scene in your life. So don't give up. Be persistent!

THE PROMISE FOR THOSE WHO PERSIST

Jesus taught the importance of persistence through a parable in Luke 11:5-13. The friend in the story has gone to bed. All the kiddos have been tucked in, the lights turned out, and the doors locked. At midnight there is a knock at the door. The friend groans and bellows from his bed, "Don't bother me. I can't get up and give you anything." But his neighbor keeps knocking on the door. Finally, the friend gets out of bed and gives the man what he wants so that he can return to bed in peace.

This parable teaches that we are to keep pounding on heaven's door when the answers to our prayers are not immediately met. Why? Because God honors persistence. He promises, "Ask and it will be given to you; seek and you will find; knock and the door will be opened to you" (verse 9). According to author Bob Sorge, "The verb tense could be translated like this: 'Ask, and keep on asking; seek, and keep on seeking; knock and keep on knocking.'"[5]

Our persistence delights the Father's heart, and the promise given is that if we persist, He *will* answer — according to His timetable and what is best. God delights in giving good gifts to His children. Sometimes the answer will not be what we want, however, but what He knows is best.

This parable leads me to wonder how many of our requests have not been answered because we've simply given up too quickly. God honors those who keep asking. For those who persist, He promises to:

- Receive our petitions (see Psalm 28:6-7)
- Reveal His goodness (see Lamentations 3:25-26)
- Renew our strength (see Isaiah 40:31)

- Restore our hope (see Romans 5:3-4)
- Remove our shame (see Psalm 25:3)

Are you waiting for God to answer a prayer request? Don't give up. Keep pounding on heaven's door. God promises to hear; and at just the right moment, He will answer according to what is best for you. Wait for Him to reveal His goodness.

THE POSTURES OF WAITING WELL

David wrote Psalm 37 during the time in his life when he was waiting to become king. This psalm describes five postures of the person who waits well. Let's take a look at each of these.

BOWING IN TRUST WHEN I FEEL LIKE PACING IN WORRY

> Do not fret. . . .
> Trust in the LORD and do good;
> > dwell in the land and enjoy safe pasture.
> (verses 1,3)

When we can't see what God is doing, our minds spin off a million "what ifs," and we soon get tangled in a web of worry. But worry accomplishes nothing. It's like pacing — we walk back and forth but end up nowhere. Instead, David tells us to trust.

I know what you're thinking: *That sounds great but . . . impossible! I mean, we're women. It's our job to worry!* In some ways you're right. It's natural to be concerned about those we love and care about. But it's what we do with those feelings that determines whether we are waiting well. Scripture says that when the feelings of worry come, we should exchange them for trust in God. Believe He is at work and has a plan for good, even though we can't see that plan. We can move from worry to trust by making an intentional decision to believe that God is sovereign, in control, and acting for our ultimate good. Every time feelings of worry try to overwhelm our trust, we once again choose faith, praying, "You know what is best, Lord. Help me to trust You more." God loves to answer prayers for more faith.

Andrew Murray writes, "The lower we bow, the nearer God will come and make our hearts bold to trust Him."[6] When we bow not just physically but mentally before Him and place our trust in His timing, fretting is replaced with faith.

A few months ago my nephew was sent to serve in the armed forces in Iraq. Jonathan began his service in Kuwait, but after a few weeks, his regiment had to travel into Iraq. The day Jonathan's unit moved into Iraq, his mom heard on the news that a convoy traveling into Iraq had been hit by a car bomb and that several soldiers were dead. Like any mother, her heart began to race, wondering if the unit hit was Jonathan's. Had her son been wounded or, worse yet, killed? She told me,

> This was by far the hardest thing I'd ever faced in my life. I choked back tears, imagining what it would be like to have army officials ring the doorbell, enter my home, and announce that my son was dead. When images of Jonathan lying wounded or dead came to my mind, I reminded myself that his physical body was only an envelope carrying his precious spirit. If my son were dead, he was with Christ, and I would have the assurance of knowing his heart was right with God. I mentally placed Jonathan back into the arms of God, begging Him to replace my fear with faith.

It was forty-eight hours before my sister-in-law received word that Jonathan's convoy had been hit but that he was okay.

There are no easy fixes or gimmicks to help us trust when life and death hang in the balance. But we can run into the safe shelter of our God, believing He ultimately knows what's best.

RAISING MY HANDS IN PRAISE WHEN I FEEL LIKE BITING MY NAILS

> Delight yourself in the LORD
> > and he will give you the desires of your heart.
> (verse 4)

Delighting in God begins with adoration. Praise lifts our eyes off the object or circumstances we are waiting for and focuses our sight on the beauty of the One who is sovereign and in control. The more we praise and delight in God's character, the more captivated we become by Him. His desires become our desires, and our faith is energized to believe His timing is best. Our deepest desires are met in Him rather than in the thing for which we are waiting.

When we assume the posture of praise, we verbalize our delight through words of thanksgiving and songs of worship. Though we may not feel thankful for our circumstances, we can thank Him in advance for the answers to our requests. This is our sacrifice of praise.

LAYING DOWN MY BURDEN WHEN I FEEL LIKE PICKING IT UP

> Commit your way to the LORD. (verse 5)

The word *commit* means to "roll"[7] our burden onto God. The picture painted is of a burden so heavy we cannot pick it up. Instead, it is rolled away from us like a big boulder and onto the Lord's strong shoulders.

One of the heaviest burdens women carry is the weight of knowing their children are not in right relationship with God. Kate knows this anguish:

> Of all the things I imagined our nineteen-year-old son doing, marrying a girl he had known for eight days was definitely not on the list! Jed was so immature and Heidi was also very young and not a Christian. To our surprise, Heidi embraced Christ and we breathed deeply and thought, *Maybe there is hope*. But after six months of marriage, Jed walked out on Heidi and on the marriage.
>
> Today Heidi is walking with the Lord, but we don't even know where Jed is. When I signed up for motherhood, I believed my sons would want my God. I feel myself caught in the never-ending cycle of waiting: I worry, I roll the burden onto God, I experience peace, then I worry again, the burden comes crashing back down, I roll it back to God again and then continue on.

Some of you can relate to Kate's anguish. You've been praying for your wayward child for so long. The agony of waiting bears down so heavily that at times you feel you can no longer pray. Take heart . . . the end of the story is not yet written. Continue to roll the burden of your child's faith onto the Lord in prayer. If anyone understands your pain, He does. He's had a few wayward children Himself. Continue to place your child in His strong arms. Allow the weight of your burden to fall on Him.

SITTING STILL WHEN I FEEL LIKE TAKING ACTION

> Be still before the LORD and wait
> patiently for him. (verse 7)

When we wait in stillness, we stop wrestling and worrying. Our souls are quiet. Author Andrew Murray describes it this way: "having our thoughts and wishes, our fears and hopes hushed into calm and quiet in that great peace of God which passes all understanding."[8]

While being still sounds good, it can be so very hard. Especially when we are waiting and everything in us wants to *do* something, to take things into our own hands and get the ball rolling. But before taking action, we need to ask ourselves, *Am I taking action because the Spirit of God is leading, or am I taking things into my own hands because I am sick and tired of waiting?*

When we act in haste rather than wait in peace, we can create a mess. Look at Sarah, Abraham's wife. God had promised her a son, but her biological clock had stopped ticking long ago, menopause was a memory, and still God had not given her a son. Sarah, sick of waiting, decided to take things into her own hands and help God out. So she suggested to Abraham that he go to bed with her servant, Hagar. As you might remember, Hagar got pregnant, taunting Sarah with the very thing she desired, and the foolishness of Sarah's plan came back to haunt her. The end result: years of family strife. But "the LORD was gracious. . . . Sarah became pregnant . . . *at the very time God had promised*" (Genesis 21:1-2, emphasis added). I love those words, "at the very time God had promised." Sarah was not in control of the time she would have a child. God was.

I do not want anyone to misunderstand what I am saying here, especially those who may be struggling to get pregnant. Women who are unable to conceive often ask me, "Is it wrong to take fertility drugs or to use a fertility clinic to aid in conception? Is that taking things into my own hands?" While the medical field has made extraordinary strides in this sensitive area, God's Word is silent on this issue. When God's Word is silent, I believe it becomes a matter for both husband and wife to prayerfully decide what is best. Let me show you what I mean.

Jill (mentioned earlier in chapter 3) and Greg prayed and tried for many years to conceive. When they didn't, they spent more years prayerfully considering fertility testing and adoption. However, they have not sensed God leading them to pursue either of these. To this day, God has not given them children of their own. Mother's Day, Father's Day, and baby dedications and showers still bring a fresh flood of tears. Though the pain of being childless still stings, Greg and Jill have learned the secret of a quieted soul. Jill says that when thoughts of God not answering her prayers creep into her mind, she immediately rejects these thoughts and redirects them toward thanksgiving. She even gives thanks for the good things that have come from infertility, such as the time she's been able to invest in ministry, mentoring, leading small groups, and encouraging others. If she had children, she would experience more time restraints. She says the hardest part has been dealing with others' expectations and pressure to reconsider adoption. Jill and Greg believe God has answered their prayers. They consistently invest in other people's children (including my own), believing God has given them this ministry.

Kelly and Rob also tried for years to conceive. Kelly had survived cancer, and chemotherapy left her an unlikely candidate for fertility drugs. After much prayer, both individually and together, the couple began to explore adoption possibilities. After waiting for over a year, they finally received "the call." Nine months ago Kelly flew to China to pick up their precious baby daughter.

Sandra and Carl tried for years to conceive to no avail. After much prayerful consideration and counsel from godly mentors, they inquired into medical help from a fertility clinic. After two years of testing and months of fertility drugs, Sandra conceived. Today they have a beautiful little girl affectionately called Miracle Child.

Each couple experienced the same frustrating, long wait, and each chose to handle it differently. Yet none of the couples made any decision without first praying about it and waiting on God. Each now enjoys the blessing of knowing that while they waited, they sought God's face. In each case God answered in His time and according to His will.

BOWING MY WILL WHEN I FEEL LIKE SHAKING MY FIST

> Refrain from anger and turn from wrath;
>> do not fret — it leads only to evil. (verse 8)

When you are continually being criticized or wrongfully treated and God doesn't intervene, it is easy to lose perspective as well as your cool. But while anger is a natural human response, Scripture tells us to hold back our anger because it can lead to sin. Just as a horse trainer needs to hold back a wild, agitated pony, so we need to hold back our anger. This is the principle Paul gives us when he writes, "In your anger do not sin" (Ephesians 4:26). Anger is inevitable, particularly if we are waiting for God to step in when we are being mistreated. How we handle that anger demonstrates if we are waiting well. We can express our anger to God, but we shouldn't vent it in destructive ways.

A few years ago, a pastor friend of ours was going through a challenging time in his church. He was tempted to lash out in anger because a small group in the congregation was continually criticizing him. Rumors and hate mail left him exhausted, discouraged, and frustrated. In his frustration he cried out to God for help, yet the criticism continued. As frustration grew, so did the temptation to let loose his anger, particularly from the pulpit.

One night, however, this pastor had a dream that he believes was from God. In his dream he saw a donkey. Those standing around the donkey were prodding and poking at the donkey with sticks and calling it names. The donkey remained still for a long time, not responding in any way to those taunting him. Finally, he could take it no more. The donkey snapped and began kicking those around him. The moment he began to kick, those poking him walked away saying, "See, we always knew he was a bad donkey!"

The moment he woke up, this pastor understood that he was the donkey in the dream. God was warning him that if he gave into anger instead of waiting for God to intervene, He would sacrifice his reputation in the face of his critics. Even though He felt desperate and impatient for God to answer his prayers and vindicate him, this man did not give in to anger. Looking back years later, our wise friend told us that as a result, God vindicated his integrity, and his critics gave up.

MY TIMES REST IN HIS HANDS

As you wait for what feels like forever, remember that all your days, hours, and moments are held between Jesus' two almighty, outstretched hands. One reads Alpha, the other Omega. His perspective on forever is higher than yours. Can you trust when you feel like worrying, raise your hands when you feel like biting your nails, lay down your burden when you feel like picking it up, sit still when you feel like taking action, and surrender when you feel like shaking your fist? God is waiting for just the perfect time to be gracious toward you.

NO MATTER HOW YOU FEEL, COME AND WORSHIP

*S*teve and I had been married for only one month. I had just poured out my heart and soul to my new husband, looking for comfort and understanding. My young groom stroked his chin thoughtfully, looked at me across the table, and then after a *long* pause said, "You know . . . I have absolutely *no* idea how to relate to you! You cry when you're happy, you cry when you're sad, you cry when you see a good movie, you cry when you're mad. What's with all the tears?" I remember thinking that it would be a *long* time before I confided in this husband of mine again!

Steve and I still laugh over that conversation. We have just celebrated our silver wedding anniversary, and we've both come a long way. Our marriage has become a safe place where each of us can confide in the other, with or without tears! But that didn't just happen. During our twenty-five years of marriage, our feelings for each other have gone up and down. We've had moments of feeling passionately in love and moments of feeling listlessly numb. We've experienced moments of great joy and moments of deep sorrow. We've shared moments of feeling intensely close and moments of feeling miles apart.

We both realize that no matter what our feelings are, our marriage will only be as rich and intimate as the amount of time and energy we devote to it. And so, no matter how we feel, we invest in our relationship. Both of us have made intentional choices to cultivate our love. We schedule a breakfast date together every week, travel together, Rollerblade, hike, and take walks together. We keep intimacy alive by talking and listening, sharing and caring, playing and loving. Our feelings rise and fall, but we are committed to making our marriage a priority. We understand that for our relationship to be a safe place, it will take both of us offering time, effort, and a whole lot of prayer.

Our relationship with Jesus is similar. At times we feel comforted and soothed by Him; other times we feel baffled and confused by Him. At moments we feel protected and loved; at other moments we feel stripped and exposed. How we handle these different feelings will determine how intimate our walk with Christ will become.

Throughout this book we have studied the "I am" statements of Jesus and examined how these statements correlate with our emotional needs. We have seen that in Him we can find a safe shelter when the winds of chaos blow. But in order to experience Christ in this way, we must come to Him and cultivate a sense of intimacy.

Over the last ten years, I have chased after His presence with all my strength. I certainly have not always felt up to it. But as I have chosen to run to Him rather than running away from Him, I have experienced a far deeper intimacy with Him than I had ever imagined. How have I done this? Through practicing His presence and making worship a priority. As I have come to know Him, I have been drawn to worship Him, and He has become my safe shelter.

Jesus never offered to remove us from the chaos of our lives. What He did offer was to be with us in the chaos and to shelter us from the burden of it (see Matthew 11:28-29). If you will center your life on Him and worship Him no matter how you feel, you too will experience the safe shelter of His presence.

CENTER YOUR LIFE ON HIM

Recently, my husband and I spent some time resting and relaxing near Lake Tahoe. While touring the town, I picked up a brochure that described the town with these words: "Life here is centered around the Lake, this pristine jewel. Like a blue diamond in the sky, it attracts the eye and keeps it focused until there is no turning away."[1]

What a perfect description of the life of a believer! Our lives are to center on the pristine beauty of our beloved Jesus Christ so that His loveliness so captivates us that we look at nothing else. He is to become everything to us. All of life is to revolve around knowing Him more intimately.

The chaos God allowed in my life became a catalyst, driving me to center my life completely on one thing — knowing Christ more. I became singly focused because I became completely desperate. Every other idol was stripped away and continues to be stripped away. I can now say that He is the pristine jewel in my life. The more I learn to worship Him, the more captivated I become.

Sam Storms describes being captivated and centered on Christ in this way: "I, you, we were made to be enchanted, enamored, and engrossed with God; enthralled, enraptured, and entranced with God; enravished, excited, and enticed by God; astonished, amazed, and awed by God; astounded, absorbed, and agog with God."[2]

Sarah Edwards, the wife of preacher Jonathan Edwards, also experienced God this way. This mother of eleven children lived in the 1700s, so she had none of the luxuries of modern living — electricity, a washing machine, plumbing, an automobile, or a refrigerator. Her husband traveled a lot as an evangelist, and she must have felt the weight of caring for her family and household. Just imagining her life makes me feel tired. Yet Sarah still found time to cultivate her love relationship with God, and as a result, her life centered on Jesus Christ. She wrote this about her experience in His presence:

> These words seem to come over and over in my mind;
> "My God, my all; my God, my all." The presence of God
> was so near and so real that I seemed scarcely conscious
> of anything else. I was entirely swallowed up in God,
> as my only portion, and His honor and glory was the
> object of my supreme desire and delight.[3]

She went on to describe the "sweet calmness of soul" she discovered. In His presence, the chaos of raising eleven children faded into the backdrop.

Sweet calmness of soul can be your experience as well. As you center your life on Christ and practice His presence, no matter what chaos might be brewing, you will discover His centering calm. The more you become captivated by Him alone, the more of Himself He will reveal. This is the secret of worship.

CULTIVATE THE ART OF PRIVATE WORSHIP

While corporate worship allows us to worship with others and is vital to our Christian growth, private times of worship cultivate a deep intimacy with Christ that we cannot experience otherwise. Fifteen or twenty minutes of worship in church on Sunday morning is not enough. If we're going to grow deeper in our love for our Lord, we need times of private worship when we linger in His presence.

Worship is meant to be a love exchange between the bride of Christ and her beloved, Jesus. It's not optional; it's essential. In His glorious presence, every other competing voice is hushed to a whisper. As we bask in His love, "he unties the tight knots within and settles our feelings."[4] When God commands us to worship Him, it is with our best interests in mind. He is inviting us to know and enjoy Him . . . and He understands this is exactly what we need because the more we enjoy Him, the more we will come, nestle down in His presence, and find in Him all that satisfies.

While most of us think of worship as singing songs on Sunday morning, I would like to suggest that worship is adoring God through the following actions:

- Lifting our praise
- Expressing our thanks
- Verbalizing our love
- Bowing our will

Let's take each of these elements of worship and see how we can cultivate them in our private worlds.

LIFTING OUR PRAISE

When I speak of praise, I am referring to adoring and admiring God's character. As we praise Him, we are drawn into His glorious character, and there we discover that He is more delightful and marvelous than we ever dreamed or imagined. The more we praise Him, the more He allows our experience of Him to deepen. God delights in our worship. Scripture tells us,

> "He who sacrifices thank offerings honors me,
>   and he prepares the way
>   so that I may show him the salvation of God."
> (Psalm 50:23)

Praise prepares our hearts to receive Him more fully. C. S. Lewis says it best: "It is in the process of being worshipped that God communicates His presence to men."[5]

The strength of our faith is proven by the depth of our praise. I have observed that those who have the most intimate walks with Christ are those who praise Him continually. These passionate followers of Jesus don't offer shallow praise, glibly saying, "God is good." Their praise has been refined in the crucible of deep suffering, and yet when all else has been stripped away, they triumphantly offer Him praise. Their never-ending mantra is:

> "I *will* bless the LORD at *all* times;
>> His praise shall *continually* be in my mouth."
> (Psalm 34:1, NASB, emphasis added)

Author Ruth Myers writes,

> As fire melts unrefined silver, bringing the impurities to the surface, so trials bring the "scum" to the top in your life. When you praise God in the midst of a trial, you cooperate with His plan to remove the scum; when you complain, you resist His plan and stir the impurities right back into your character.[6]

I used to wonder what I should do on the days when I didn't feel like praising God. It almost seemed hypocritical to praise God when I felt emotionally flat. But then a wise friend told me that she believes God sometimes uses our numbness to give our emotions a rest. Even if we feel nothing, we can still come to God and tell Him we feel nothing and that we yearn to experience His love again and long for the joy we once felt. We can still praise Him by faith for His goodness. Dr. John G. Mitchell, cofounder of Multnomah School of the Bible once said, "To give thanks when you don't feel like it is not hypocrisy; it's obedience."[7] So don't postpone praise until you feel better; come and praise Him now.

How do we praise? We begin by intentionally setting aside a portion of time each day to praise and adore God. This is the idea behind the

Twenty-Minute Worship Challenge. Without intention, it won't happen.

To help you get started, I recommend using a tool, such as this one mentioned in chapter 3: Use the letters of the alphabet to come up with words to describe God. Or personalize the "I am" statements of Jesus. For example: "My Light of the World, I praise You that You will guide me today" or "My Bread of Life, I praise You that You offer me all the love I could ever imagine. I praise You that the supply of Your love never runs out and that I can come and eat till my heart is full." You can also use the psalms or other passages of Scripture, such as the doxologies Paul wrote in some of his epistles. When we use Scripture in our praise, our voices are brought into unison with the Holy Spirit's voice. Together we resonate praise to the Lord Jesus Christ with one voice.

Recently, I asked a group what they use to prompt their praise. Here are some of their ideas:

- My daughter Bethany loves to run, so she uses her daily running time to worship. She puts on a headset with worship music to prompt her thoughts toward praise. As she runs, savoring the beauty of God's creation all around her, she expresses her praise to the Lord.

- Jeanne lights a candle and worships. The candle draws her focus upward toward Jesus as the Light of the World.

- Angela puts a chair in the room and envisions Jesus sitting in it. Then kneeling before the chair, Angela brings herself to a place of absolute quiet before she begins verbalizing her praise.

- Gracie worships through her art. She created an entire scrapbook prompted by the attributes of God.

- Rachelle journals as an act of worship. She writes love letters that express her desire to know Christ more deeply.

When we become intentional about praise, it becomes easier to praise God all day long. This has become my goal. I long to become a woman of praise, no matter what chaos might exist in my life. I have a bracelet that I wear to remind me to praise Him all day long. Throughout the day, whenever I see or feel that bracelet, I immediately choose to praise Christ for some quality of His character, whether I feel like it or not.

I have discovered that if I am faithful in choosing praise, my feelings will follow. All of a sudden, I find myself flooded with feelings of thanksgiving, the second element of worship.

EXPRESSING OUR THANKS

Thanksgiving is the overflow of a grateful heart, but thankfulness needs to be cultivated. When our children were very small, we were often invited over to our parishioners' houses for dinner. I got tired of turning to my children as we were leaving and asking, "What do you say?" in an effort to prompt a "thank you." So, I offered our children an incentive. On our way to dinner, I told them, "If you remember to say, 'Thank you for the lovely dinner' without a reminder from me, I will give you a quarter." Money speaks! (Now that they're older, I'd probably have to offer twenty bucks!) While some might call that bribery, this incentive cultivated gratefulness in my children, and even after they outgrew the quarter, the habit stuck, and they remembered on their own to thank hostesses for dinner. So it is in our walk with God — thankfulness needs to be cultivated, but it can become a habit.

Psalm 100:4 teaches us that we are to enter His gates with thanksgiving. Christ has done so much for us. He's offered us His unconditional love. He's saved us and given us His grace. He's offered us cleansing, love, guidance, hope, and much more. He's provided for our needs and even many of our wants. How can we do less than offer Him thanksgiving?

My husband keeps a list in his journal of things for which he is thankful. I decided to try out his idea with a friend of mine who lived across the country. Both of us were in a challenging time in our lives. During the ten days before Thanksgiving, we agreed to come up with a list of ten new things we were thankful for every day and send that list to each other via e-mail. We could not repeat any of the things on each other's list. By Thanksgiving we each had a list of one hundred things we were thankful for. And more important, both of our spirits had been lifted because we had cultivated attitudes of thanksgiving. The more we learn to thank God, the more our hearts will be filled with love for Him.

VERBALIZING OUR LOVE

Part of worship is verbalizing our love for God. To some this feels foreign. But as we learn to express our love for Him, we find that we begin to feel His love in return.

How do we verbalize love to God when we can't see Him, touch Him, or hear His audible voice? I believe we can do this by using terms of endearment with Him. When we begin our prayers with phrases such as *My Beloved Jesus*, *My Loving Abba*, or *Precious Holy One*, we cultivate feelings of love and safety between Him and us. He is our eternal bridegroom, and as we express our love for Him, we begin to feel the security of His divine embrace. Author Dana Candler notes, "Oh how safe is the dwelling place of God! Oh how secure is the bride of His choice in the treasured place of His embrace! And oh, the pleasure of His embrace!"[8]

When we express our love in worship, we might pray something like this:

> My beloved Jesus, I love You this morning. I'm here
> to worship You. Show me today how to bring pleasure

to You. I adore You. You alone are my heart's deepest desire. Show me how to love You more. You have been so good to me. Your grace and love are beyond anything I can imagine. I want to know more of You. I want to know You as intimately as I can. Please reveal more of Yourself to me because I want to love You more. Holy Spirit, bring my spirit into perfect union with Yours so that my heart will become one with Yours.

BOWING OUR WILL

While praise is perhaps the greatest privilege of believers, surrender is perhaps the highest form of worship. As we bow before God, we give Him everything we might grasp. Our pride, our reputation, our health, our identity, our loved ones — we place all at His feet in favor of clinging solely to Him. As Ruth Myers explains, "In genuine spiritual worship, we bow before the Most High God, the most merciful and reliable and winsome of all beings, and we crown Him as Lord of all that we are."[9]

This is a process in our lives. In a life of worship, we bow continually, surrendering until He calls us home. Years ago my husband had the opportunity to officiate at the funeral of a godly woman who had struggled for years with arthritis. Crippled and confined to a wheelchair, Betty wrote these words near the end of her life:

Lord I am willing

> To receive what you give
> To lack what you withhold
> To relinquish what you take
> To suffer what you inflict
> To be what you require
>
>> Signed: Betty

Her husband, who has now gone home to be with the Lord, gave that paper to Steve. As a couple we've returned to Betty's covenant many times in order to remind ourselves that we must bow and surrender our will to His. This is the highest form of worship.

God is calling you to center your life on Jesus Christ and to cultivate the practice of private worship. How will you respond? Don't wait until you feel like it.

NO MATTER HOW YOU FEEL, COME

After Jesus left the disciples and ascended, the disciples "worshiped him and returned to Jerusalem with great joy" (Luke 24:52). I love the pattern I see in this verse. Joy came after worship. The chaos in their lives didn't dissipate, but something in them had changed because they had worshiped.

We cannot escape the chaos of life either. But no matter what is going on in our lives, we can continually run into the safe shelter of His presence and find calmness and joy. As we worship Him, the clamor grows dimmer because our attention is drawn up into His loveliness. No longer are we focused on the enormity of the chaos but on the extraordinariness of our "I am," who invites:

> Come My beloved . . .
> Come hungry and needy,
> Come lonely and afraid,
> Come angry and hurt,
> Come anxious and frazzled,
> But come.
> Exalt Me as I Am,
> For I alone am able to meet your deepest needs.

INTRODUCTION TO TWELVE-WEEK BIBLE STUDY

Dear Friend,

I am excited that you have joined me in this study of Jesus and His "I am" statements. While studying the Bible will help you *know* God's character, memorizing, meditating, and worshiping will help you *experience* His character because these disciplines help the truth of His character to travel from your head down into your heart. For this reason, each of the twelve lessons includes a portion of Scripture for you to memorize, and ten of the lessons include a daily worship challenge designed to help you experience His presence through twenty minutes of praise and thanksgiving each day. Both of these spiritual disciplines will deepen your experience of God's presence. Don't worry if you miss a day or two; just get back on track the next day and continue.

These lessons can be done individually, with a friend, or in a small group. Because some of the topics in the book are private and personal, I recommend that each person doing this study in a group agree to a covenant of confidentiality. This will help everyone in the group to feel assured that her story will not be told outside the group. Also keep in mind that while vulnerability is admirable, no one participating in a group study should feel pressured to divulge details of her personal story beyond what she is comfortable sharing. Agree together to respect each other's boundaries.

My prayer for you is that by the end of the twelve weeks, you will have buried yourself in the heart of Jesus and experienced calm in the safe shelter of His presence.

I AM PRAYING FOR YOU,
BECKY HARLING

WEEK ONE

Read chapter 1, "Nowhere to Run, Nowhere to Hide."

1. Memorize and meditate on Psalm 91:1-2, as written here or in another translation.

> He who dwells in the shelter of the Most High
>> will rest in the shadow of the Almighty.
> I will say of the LORD, "He is my refuge and my fortress,
>> my God, in whom I trust."

2. Describe how it would feel to be nestled under the wings of the Almighty. Do you think that peace is possible in your life at this time? Why or why not?

3. Which most often describes you: calm and collected, like the person in Jeremiah 17:7-8, or fried and frazzled? Why?

4. What challenges are you facing in your life right now? Describe them here.

5. Read over the list of "I am" statements in the table of contents. To which statement are you most drawn? Why?

6. What do you hope to gain by reading this book and doing the correlating Bible study?

7. Write a prayer to Jesus thanking Him that He longs to be your safe shelter.

WEEK TWO

Read chapter 2, "Where Can I Dump My Bucket of Guilt?"

1. Memorize 1 John 1:9, as written here or in another translation.

   If we confess our sins, he is faithful and just and
   will forgive us our sin and purify us from all
   unrighteousness.

2. Below is a scale from one to ten. Circle the number that best represents how full your bucket of guilt is. On this scale, one represents hardly any guilt at all, and ten represents a bucket of guilt that's overflowing.

   1   2   3   4   5   6   7   8   9   10

3. Read and meditate on James 2:10.

   a. Write your own definition of true guilt.

   b. Describe why you need a Messiah.

4. Write your own definition of false guilt.

5. List the top three things that you feel guilty for. Then evaluate each one and decide whether it is true or false guilt.

6. Read and meditate on 1 Corinthians 6:11. Personalize this verse, substituting "I was" for "you were." Write your personalized version here.

7. Read and meditate on 1 Thessalonians 4:3 and 1 Thessalonians 5:23. To be sanctified means to be made clean. Do you feel clean? Why or why not?

8. The next time you feel guilty, what will you do to experience safe shelter in Jesus?

9. After reading this chapter, how would you explain to a friend that he or she needs a Messiah? Write your thoughts here.

WEEK THREE

Read chapter 3, "I Want to Feel Loved!"

1. Do the Twenty-Minute Worship Challenge every day this week. Focus on Christ's love. At the end of the week, summarize your reflections here.

2. Memorize Ephesians 3:17-19, as written here or in another translation.

> And I pray that you, being rooted and established in love, may have power, together with all the saints, to grasp how wide and long and high and deep is the love of Christ, and to know this love that surpasses knowledge — that you may be filled to the measure of all the fullness of God.

3. Read and meditate on Psalm 63:1-5. This prayer, written by David, expresses his hunger to experience more of God's love. Write a prayer here, describing how hungry you are to experience Christ's love.

4. Describe the last time you felt deeply loved by God. Where were you? What were you doing? What were your feelings?

5. Reflect on this truth: Our emotions don't dictate the truth of God's love. But God wants the truth of His love to penetrate our emotions. What does this statement mean to you personally?

6. Read and meditate on Isaiah 43:4. This verse describes how God feels about you! Paraphrase this verse, personalizing it and including your name. For example: "Becky, you are precious . . ."

7. Make a list of twenty-six adjectives that describe God's love using each letter of the alphabet. For example: God's love is awesome, boundless, compassionate . . .

8. Write a prayer of thanksgiving using some of the adjectives you just listed to praise Christ for His love for you.

WEEK FOUR

Read chapter 4, "Hey, I Need a Little Direction Here!"

1. Do the Twenty-Minute Worship Challenge every day this week. Focus on Jesus as your light and guide. At the end of the week, summarize your reflections here.

2. Memorize Proverbs 3:5-6, as written here or in another translation.

> Trust in the LORD with all your heart
>   and lean not on your own understanding;
> in all your ways acknowledge him,
>   and he will make your paths straight.

3. Where do you need Christ's guidance at this moment in your life?

4. Read the section in the chapter titled "Set Your Heart to Follow" and then read Psalm 40:8.

   a. How would you describe David's attitude in this psalm?

b. Which word best describes your attitude when following Christ's leading: *ready* or *reluctant*? Why?

5. How would your life be different if you sought to know the will of the Lord before making any decisions?

6. What does it mean for you personally to cultivate a heart that relinquishes?

7. Read and meditate on Psalm 119:105. How is God's Word a light to your feet?

8. Read Luke 1:46 and Psalm 34:3. In your words, write out what it means for you to bring God glory.

WEEK FIVE

Read chapter 5, "Where Do I Hide When I'm Petrified?"

1. Do the Twenty-Minute Worship Challenge every day this week. Focus on Jesus as your Good Shepherd. At the end of the week, summarize your reflections here.

2. Memorize Psalm 23, as written here or in another translation.

> The LORD is my shepherd, I shall not be in want.
>   He makes me lie down in green pastures,
> he leads me beside quiet waters,
>   he restores my soul.
> He guides me in paths of righteousness
>   for his name's sake.
> Even though I walk
>   through the valley of the shadow of death,
> I will fear no evil,
>   for you are with me;
> your rod and your staff,
>   they comfort me.
> You prepare a table before me
>   in the presence of my enemies.
> You anoint my head with oil;
>   my cup overflows.

Surely goodness and love will follow me
all the days of my life,
and I will dwell in the house of the LORD
forever.

3. Read John 10:11-15. List all the differences between the Good Shepherd and the hired hand. Then write how it quiets your fears to know you belong to the Good Shepherd.

4. Read Isaiah 40:11. This verse is a prophecy concerning Jesus as the Good Shepherd. What are the qualities of the Good Shepherd as mentioned in this verse?

5. Read Matthew 18:10-14. How are the qualities of the Good Shepherd described in Isaiah 40:11 seen in the parable of the lost sheep?

6. Read John 10:27-28. How do you personally listen for the Shepherd's voice? How does His voice calm your fears? What does it mean to you that no one can snatch you out of His hand?

7. Look over the six promises in Psalm 23 that are listed below. For each one, write a sentence describing how that promise quiets a fear you have recently struggled with.

   a. He promises to provide for your needs (verse 1).

   b. He promises to restore your soul (verse 3).

   c. He promises to guide you (verse 3).

   d. He promises to be with you in your dark valley (verse 4).

e. He promises to comfort you when you face evil (verse 5).

f. He promises to hold you secure in the future (verse 6).

8. What is your worst fear?

   a. Describe how knowing the Shepherd's character quiets that fear.

   b. Turn your panic to praise by writing a personal prayer thanking the Shepherd that He knows your fear and will take care of it in His time and His way. Praise Him that you can trust Him.

WEEK SIX

Read chapter 6, "How Do I Rekindle Hope?"

1. Do the Twenty-Minute Worship Challenge every day this week. Focus on Jesus as your personal hope. At the end of the week, summarize your reflections here.

2. Memorize Psalm 42:11, as written here or in another translation.

> Why are you downcast, O my soul?
>   Why so disturbed within me?
> Put your hope in God,
>   for I will yet praise him,
>   my Savior and my God.

3. Has there ever been a time when God seemed aloof to you? Write about it here.

4. Read and meditate on Psalm 56:8 and John 11:35. How do you think God feels about your tears?

5. Read Luke 7:36-48 and 1 Samuel 1:10. Reflect on the tears both women shed. How can we worship God when we are weeping?

6. Define hope using your own words. What does it mean to you to center your hope on Jesus Christ?

7. Reflect on this quote by Joni Eareckson Tada: "Heartache forces us to embrace God out of desperate, urgent need. God is never closer than when your heart is aching."[1] Do you agree or disagree with this statement? Why?

8. Read and meditate on Jeremiah 29:11.

    a. Paraphrase this verse in the space that follows.

    b. If you believed this truth, how would your life be different?

WEEK SEVEN

Read chapter 7, "Where Can I Go to Feel At Home?"

1. Do the Twenty-Minute Worship Challenge every day this week. Focus your praise on Jesus as the way to find intimate belonging. At the end of the week, summarize your reflections here.

2. Memorize John 14:1,6, as written here or in another translation.

> "Do not let your hearts be troubled. Trust in God; trust also in me." . . .
> Jesus answered, "I am the way and the truth and the life. No one comes to the Father except through me."

3. How does knowing Jesus as the Way provide a sense of belonging for you personally?

4. Read over Hudson Taylor's words on page 109. What are your deep soul yearnings? Write them here. How have you tried to fill these longings in the past?

5. Paraphrase Psalm 63:1-5 in the space that follows.

6. Jesus told the disciples it was better for them that He go away and leave the Holy Spirit (see John 16:7).

    a. Why is it better for you to have the Holy Spirit living in you than Jesus' physical presence on the earth?

    b. How does the Holy Spirit enable you to feel at home with God?

    c. Look back over the roles the Holy Spirit plays in our lives on page 112. When was the last time you experienced the Holy Spirit's presence in your life? Describe how you felt His presence.

7. When was the last time you enjoyed some quality time alone? How did you spend that time?

8. Read Ephesians 2:10. You are God's special poem. What are the gifts and abilities God has given you? How would you describe your God-given personality?

9. Think about the relationships you enjoy. Using the five concentric circles depicted on page 122, develop an intentional plan for spending time in community this week. For example:

   Circle A — Spend a half hour each morning alone with God in Bible reading and prayer.

   Circle B — Take a walk with my husband and listen to his heart. Or spend quality time with one of my children or my aging parent.

WEEK EIGHT

Read chapter 8, "Please, Set Me Free!"

1. Do the Twenty-Minute Worship Challenge every day this week. Focus your praise on the freedom you have in Christ. At the end of the week, summarize your reflections here.

2. Memorize John 8:32,36, as written here or in another translation.

> "Then you will know the truth, and the truth will set you free. . . .
> So if the Son sets you free, you will be free indeed."

3. Look over the types of lies that we embrace described in chapter 8. Which lie do you most often embrace?

4. Write an answer for each of the following questions. Be specific.

   a. How would your view of your body change if you embraced God's truth about your body?

b. How would your spending change if you embraced God's truth about your spending habits?

c. How would your behavior change if you embraced God's truth about your sexuality?

d. How would your behavior change if you embraced God's truth about your gossip?

5. Plan your own private escape route.

a. Reveal: Read and meditate on 2 Corinthians 4:2. Answer the four questions listed on page 138.

b. Remove: Write down three personal goals that will help you remove yourself from your temptation magnet.

c. Reclothe: Select a Scripture from the list at the end of chapter 8 that addresses the lie you most often embrace. Personalize that Scripture in prayer in the space below.

d. Restore: Prayerfully begin seeking God for an accountability partner. If possible, make contact with that person this week and set a time when you will meet.

6. Read and meditate on Galatians 5:1.

a. Paraphrase this verse in the space that follows. Then write a prayer to the Lord using the words of this verse.

b. What does it look like for you personally to "stand firm" and not allow yourself to become entangled again?

7. No matter what has held you captive, Jesus calls you to surrender. Write your own prayer of surrender here.

WEEK NINE

Read chapter 9, "But I Can't!"

1. Do the Twenty-Minute Worship Challenge every day this week. Focus on Jesus as the Vine. At the end of the week, summarize your reflections here.

2. Memorize Philippians 4:13, as written here or in another translation.

   I can do everything through him who gives me strength.

3. Read John 15:1-10 at least twice and meditate on Jesus' words. Count and circle each time Jesus instructs the disciples to abide (or remain, in some translations) and then write the number here: _____. Now write your own definition for abiding in Christ.

4. Paraphrase John 15:4 in the space that follows. According to this verse, what is the condition for fruitfulness?

5. How have you usurped the role of the Vine recently? How would the situation have been different if you had allowed Christ to be the Vine? Write about it here.

6. Read Hebrews 12:5-6. According to these verses, why does the Father discipline or prune His children?

7. Have you experienced God's pruning recently? How has that pruning produced more of the fruit of holiness in your life?

8. Read and meditate on Galatians 5:22-23. List the fruit of the Spirit here. Choose one to focus on this week. Write a prayer asking the Gardener to cultivate that attitude in your life this week.

9. If you were to partner with God this week and allow the Holy Spirit to flow through you to others, what in your life would change?

WEEK TEN

Read chapter 10, "How Much Longer, Lord?"

1. Do the Twenty-Minute Worship Challenge every day this week. Praise Jesus that His timing in your life is perfect. At the end of the week, summarize your reflections here.

2. Memorize Psalm 37:3-5, as written here or in another translation.

> Trust in the LORD and do good;
>> dwell in the land and enjoy safe pasture.
> Delight yourself in the LORD
>> and he will give you the desires of your heart.
> Commit your way to the LORD;
>> trust in him and he will do this.

3. What prayer are you waiting for God to answer right now? Write about it here.

4. "Delay never thwarts God's purpose; rather it polishes His instrument."[2] What are your thoughts on this quote? How has God used delay to "polish" you?

5. Read Luke 11:9. Does this verse mean that if we persist, God will give us all that we desire? Why or why not? What does this verse teach you about persistence in prayer?

6. Write a definition for trust using your own words. What does it look like for you to trust God when He seems silent?

7. Meditate on Psalm 37:4.

    a. How do you express your delight in the Lord?

    b. What is your heart's deepest desire?

    c. Write a prayer of thanksgiving praising Jesus that you can trust Him with your desires.

8. What are the burdens you are feeling most heavily at this time? List them here. How can you roll these burdens onto the Lord?

WEEK ELEVEN

Read the conclusion, "No Matter How You Feel, Come and Worship."

1. Do the Twenty-Minute Worship Challenge every day this week. Do you think this has been an important exercise to help you experience Christ as your safe shelter? Why or why not?

2. Memorize Philippians 2:9-11, as written here or in another translation.

> Therefore God exalted him to the highest place and gave him the name that is above every name, that at the name of Jesus every knee should bow, in heaven and on earth and under the earth, and every tongue confess that Jesus Christ is Lord, to the glory of God the Father.

3. Define worship in your own words.

4. Read and meditate on Psalm 100.

   a. How are we to enter God's presence?

   b. What are some ways we can express praise that are listed in this psalm? Write them here.

5. Read and meditate on Philippians 3:8.

   a. Paraphrase this verse in the space that follows.

   b. How would your behavior change if your one compelling desire was to know Christ better?

6. Sarah Edwards felt "sweet calmness of soul" in the presence of Christ. What prevents you from feeling that calmness in your worship time?

7. "To give thanks when you don't feel like it is not hypocrisy; it's obedience."[3] What are your personal reflections on this quote? What do you do in your worship time to cultivate an attitude of praise when you don't feel like giving thanks? Write your thoughts here.

8. Read and meditate on Luke 7:36-39.

    a. Describe this woman's worship.

    b. What is the most extravagant way you can think of to express your love to Jesus? Write about it here.

9. If you had three minutes to convince a friend to begin the art of personal worship, what would you say?

WEEK TWELVE

1. Do the Twenty-Minute Worship Challenge, but set aside one day to spend a longer amount of time in worship. Ask the Holy Spirit to bring to your mind all you have learned through this study and praise Jesus for what you have learned and the ways you have grown.

2. Memorize and meditate on Hebrews 1:3, as written here or in another translation.

   The Son is the radiance of God's glory and the exact representation of his being, sustaining all things by his powerful word.

3. According to this verse and based on our study of each of the "I am" statements of Jesus, who is Jesus Christ?

4. Reflect on each of the "I am" statements. Which statement meant the most to you? Why? Write your reflections here.

5. How have you changed through this study? How has your understanding of God's character changed?

6. If you were to describe to a friend how Jesus has become your safe shelter, what would you say? Write your thoughts here.

7. How did the Twenty-Minute Worship Challenge enable you to experience the presence of God?

8. Why would you recommend this book and study to a friend?

NOTES

FOREWORD

1. Richard J. Foster, *Prayer: Finding the Heart's True Home* (San Francisco: HarperCollins, 1992), 252–253.

CHAPTER 2: WHERE CAN I DUMP MY BUCKET OF GUILT?

1. When Israel's northern kingdom fell captive to the Assyrians (722 BC), many Israelites intermarried with the Assyrians. The Samaritans were their descendants.

2. Bruce B. Barton and others, *Life Application Bible Commentary* (Wheaton, Ill.: Tyndale, 1993), 88.

3. C. H. Spurgeon, *The Treasury of David*, vol. 1 (McLean, Va.: MacDonald Publishing Company, n.d.), 416.

CHAPTER 3: I WANT TO FEEL LOVED!

1. Philip W. Comfort and Wendell C. Hawley, *Opening the Gospel of John* (Wheaton, Ill.: Tyndale, 1994), 111.

2. Sam Storms, *The Singing God* (Lake Mary, Fla.: Creation House, 1998), 126.

3. Ruth Myers, *The Satisfied Heart* (Colorado Springs, Colo.: WaterBrook, 1999), 107.

4. Sam Storms, *Pleasures Evermore* (Colorado Springs, Colo.: NavPress, 2000), 211.

CHAPTER 4: HEY, I NEED A LITTLE DIRECTION HERE!

1. *Discipleship Journal*, no. 134 (March/April 2003).

2. W. E. Vine, *An Expository Dictionary of New Testament Words* (Old Tappan, N.J.: Revell, 1966), III.

3. Alan Redpath, *The Making of a Man of God* (Old Tappan, N.J.: Revell, 1962), 93.

4. C. H. Spurgeon, *The Treasury of David*, vol. 3 (McLean, Va.: MacDonald Publishing Company, n.d.), 40.

5. John Piper, *Desiring God* (Portland, Oreg.: Multnomah, 1986), 43.

6. Erwin McManus, *Seizing Your Divine Moment* (Nashville: Nelson, 2002), 90.

7. Stormie Omartian, *Just Enough Light for the Step I'm On* (Eugene, Oreg.: Harvest House, 1999), 44.

CHAPTER 5: WHERE DO I HIDE WHEN I'M PETRIFIED?

1. Dorothy Kelley Patterson, ed., *The Women's Study Bible*, Chart on Names of God (Nashville: Nelson, 1995), 861.

2. Patterson, 861.

3. Max Lucado, *Traveling Light* (Nashville: W Publishing, 2001), 15.

4. Max Lucado, *Safe in the Shepherd's Arms* (Nashville: J. Countryman, 2002), 19.

5. John Piper, "George Mueller's Strategy for Showing God: Simplicity of Faith, Sacred Scripture, Satisfaction in God," *Desiring God*, February 3, 2004, www.desiringgod.org/library/biographies/04mueller.html.

6. Phillip Keller, *A Shepherd Looks at Psalm 23* (Minneapolis: Worldwide Publications, 1970), 60.

7. Keller, 72.

8. Matthew Henry, *Matthew Henry's Commentary*, vol. 2 (Wilmington, Del.: Sovereign Grace Publishers, 1972), 1283.

9. Keller, 72.

10. Keller, 94.

11. Keller, 99.

12. Donald Seltzer, "Keep On." All rights reserved by Hidden Life, Inc. Used with permission.

CHAPTER 6: HOW DO I REKINDLE HOPE?

1. Carol Kent, *When I Lay My Isaac Down* (Colorado Springs, Colo.: NavPress, 2004), 61.

2. Larry Crabb, *Shattered Dreams: God's Unexpected Pathway to Joy* (Colorado Springs, Colo.: WaterBrook, 2001), 144.

3. Anne Graham Lotz, *My Heart's Cry* (Nashville: W Publishing, 2002), 26.

4. Jess Moody, quoted by Lloyd Cory, *Quotable Quotes* (Wheaton, Ill.: Victor, 1985), 76.

5. Joni Eareckson Tada and Steven Estes, *When God Weeps* (Grand Rapids, Mich.: Zondervan, 1997).

6. Tada and Estes, 65.

7. J. R. Miller, quoted in Mrs. Charles E. Cowman, *Streams in the Desert* (Grand Rapids, Mich.: Zondervan, 1984), March 15 entry.

CHAPTER 7: WHERE CAN I GO TO FEEL AT HOME?

1. Hudson Taylor, quoted in Ruth Myers, *The Satisfied Heart* (Colorado Springs, Colo.: WaterBrook, 1999), 41.

2. Lloyd John Ogilvie, *The Bush Is Still Burning* (Waco, Tex.: Word, 1980), 163.

3. Linda Dillow, *Calm My Anxious Heart* (Colorado Springs, Colo.: NavPress, 1998), 37.

4. John MacArthur, *The MacArthur New Testament Commentary: Ephesians* (Chicago: Moody, 1986), 63.

5. Ogilvie, 165.

CHAPTER 8: PLEASE, SET ME FREE!

1. Lloyd John Ogilvie, *The Bush Is Still Burning* (Waco, Tex.: Word, 1980), 172.

2. Marian Eberly (RN, LCSW, DAPA, vice president of Patient Care Services), in an interview with the author, September 23, 2004.

3. W. E. Vine, *An Expository Dictionary of New Testament Words*, vol. 4 (Old Tappan, N.J.: Revell, 1966), 39.

4. Amy Carmichael, *Edges of His Ways* (Fort Washington, Pa.: Christian Literature Crusade, 1955), 113.

5. Francis Frangipane, *Holiness, Truth and the Presence of God* (Cedar Rapids, Iowa: Arrow Publications, 1986), 60.

CHAPTER 9: BUT I CAN'T

1. Andrew Murray, *The True Vine* (New Kensington, Pa.: Whitaker House, 1982), 12.

2. Roy Heisson, "I Am the True Vine," *Discipleship Journal*, no. 118 (November/December, 2000), 69.

3. Bruce Wilkinson, *Secrets of the Vine* (Sisters, Oreg.: Multnomah, 2001), 33.

4. Cynthia Heald, *Abiding in Christ* (Colorado Springs, Colo.: NavPress, 1995), 9.

5. Brennan Manning, "How I Keep Growing," *Discipleship Journal*, no. 118 (July/August 2000), 59.

6, Wilkinson, 104.

7. Brother Lawrence, quoted in Wilkinson, 110.

CHAPTER 10: HOW MUCH LONGER, LORD?

1. V. Raymond Edman, *The Disciplines of Life* (Wheaton, Ill.: Victor, 1948), 80.

2. Bob Sorge, *The Fire of Delayed Answers* (Greenwood, Miss.: Oasis House, 1996), 61.

3. Sorge, 62.
4. Dr. and Mrs. Howard Taylor, *Hudson Taylor's Spiritual Secret* (London: China Inland Mission, 1935), 75.
5. Sorge, 92.
6. Andrew Murray, *Waiting on God* (Springdale, Pa.: Whitaker House, 1981), 49.
7. C. H. Spurgeon, *The Treasury of David*, vol. 1 (McLean, Va.: MacDonald Publishing Company, n.d.), 171.
8. Murray, 52.

CONCLUSION: NO MATTER HOW YOU FEEL, COME AND WORSHIP
1. Tammy Thompson, "Summer in Lake Tahoe," *Sunny Day Guide to Lake Tahoe* 9, no. 2 (2003): 11.
2. Sam Storms, *Pleasures Evermore* (Colorado Springs, Colo.: NavPress, 2000), 107.
3. Jonathan Edwards, *The Works of Jonathan Edwards*, vol. 1 (Edinburgh: Banner of Truth, 1979), lxii–lxx.
4. Ruth Myers, *31 Days of Praise* (Sisters, Oreg.: Multnomah, 1994), 29.
5. C. S. Lewis, *Reflections on the Psalms* (New York: Harcourt, Brace and World, 1958), 90–98.
6. Myers, 127.
7. Dr. John G. Mitchell as quoted in Myers, 27.
8. Dana Candler, *Deep Unto Deep* (n.p.: Forerunner Publishing, 2004), 63.
9. Myers, 23.

TWELVE-WEEK BIBLE STUDY
1. Joni Eareckson Tada and Steven Estes, *When God Weeps* (Grand Rapids, Mich.: Zondervan, 1997), 65.
2. V. Raymond Edman, *The Disciplines of Life* (Wheaton, Ill.: Victor, 1948), 80.

3. Dr. John G. Mitchell as quoted in Ruth Myers, *31 Days of Praise* (Sisters, Oreg.: Multnomah, 1994), 27.

ABOUT THE AUTHOR

*B*ecky Harling and her husband, Steve, have served in pastoral ministry for twenty-five years both in the United States and overseas.

A frequent speaker at conferences and women's events, Becky is passionate about seeing the Word of God come alive in the hearts of women and watching women grow deeper in their walk with Jesus Christ. She has extensive experience in women's ministry and small-group ministry. Becky and Steve are the parents of four children ranging in age from fourteen to twenty-three.

Recently, the Harlings moved to Monument, Colorado to launch Radiance International, an organization that creatively partners churches with mission agencies to launch strategic global initiatives.

FOCUS ON GOD,
NOT THE CIRCUMSTANCES.

Calm My Anxious Heart

The truth is, it's easier to worry than to trust God. This book includes a twelve-week study, which combined with the companion journal will help women focus on growing in contentment and faith.

Linda Dillow   1-57683-047-0

Calm My Anxious Heart: My Mercies Journal

Linda Dillow   1-57683-116-7

The Blessing Book

When we find ourselves in the valley, we must remember to turn our eyes away from the suffering and toward the Healer—He can make it a place of blessing.

Linda Dillow   1-57683-464-6

Visit your local Christian bookstore, call NavPress at 1-800-366-7788, or log on to www.navpress.com to purchase.

To locate a Christian bookstore near you, call 1-800-991-7747.

NAVPRESS
BRINGING TRUTH TO LIFE
www.navpress.com